T0149523

OTHER BOOKS BY
STEVEN DOUGLAS GLOVER

A Shiny Christmas Star; An Old West Christmas Trilogy

The Stockton Saga: Dawn of the Gunfighter

The Stockton Saga 2; Star of Justice

The Stockton Saga 3; A Man to Reckon With

The Stockton Saga 4; The Lady From Colorado

Lady Wears a Star

Steven Douglas Glover

 iUniverse®

LADY WEARS A STAR

Copyright © 2017 Steven Douglas Glover.

All rights reserved. No part of this book may be used or reproduced by any means,
graphic, electronic, or mechanical, including photocopying, recording, taping or by
any information storage retrieval system without the written permission of the author
except in the case of brief quotations embodied in critical articles and reviews.

Certain characters in this work are historical figures, and certain events portrayed did take place.
However, this is a work of fiction. All of the other characters, names, and events as well as all
places, incidents, organizations, and dialogue in this novel are either the products of the author's
imagination or are used fictitiously. If there are only a few historical figures or actual events in
the novel, the disclaimer could name them: For example: "Edwin Stanton and Salmon Chase
are historical figures..." or "The King and Queen of Burma were actually exiled by the British
in 1885." The rest of the disclaimer would follow: However, this is a work of fiction. All of the
other characters, names, and events as well as all places, incidents, organizations, and dialogue
in this novel are either are the products of the author's imagination or are used fictitiously.

iUniverse books may be ordered through booksellers or by contacting:

iUniverse
1663 Liberty Drive
Bloomington, IN 47403
www.iuniverse.com
1-800-Authors (1-800-288-4677)

Because of the dynamic nature of the Internet, any web addresses or links contained in
this book may have changed since publication and may no longer be valid. The views
expressed in this work are solely those of the author and do not necessarily reflect the
views of the publisher, and the publisher hereby disclaims any responsibility for them.

Any people depicted in stock imagery provided by Thinkstock are models,
and such images are being used for illustrative purposes only.
Certain stock imagery © Thinkstock.

ISBN: 978-1-5320-3624-8 (sc)
ISBN: 978-1-5320-3625-5 (e)

Print information available on the last page.

iUniverse rev. date: 11/09/2017

CONTENTS

Preface vii
U.S. Marshal Quotation.. ix
Dedication Page xi

Chapter One: A Parting of Friends... 1
Chapter Two: A Grim Discovery... 7
Chapter Three: A Hard Decision... 13
Chapter Four: Justice Finds the Guilty...19
Chapter FIve: Strange Lady in Town.. 25
Chapter Six: A New Star for Justice... 31
Chapter Seven: Training the New Deputy Marshal... 39
Chapter Eight: A Horse for Lydia... 49
Chapter Nine: Serving Writs and Warrants.. 57
Chapter Ten: A Murderer Escapes 65
Chapter Eleven: Gabe Johnson... 73
Chapter Twelve: Lydia's Reward 79
Chapter Thirteen: Visions of Early Life 85
Chapter Fourteen: Into The Nations 99
Chapter Fifteen: An Interesting Testimony 107
Chapter Sixteen: An Old Friend.. 115
Chapter Seventeen: Ride to McAlester 127
Chapter Eighteen: A Dangerous Road to Paris 135
Chapter Nineteen: Corbin Morgan 143
Chapter Twenty: A Party of Marshals 155
Chapter Twenty-One: McAlester Federal Jail 165
Chapter Twenty-Two: Justice.. 173

PREFACE

Some years ago, I waited anxiously for my long anticipated History Channel program to start. It was entitled, *U.S. Marshals, The Old West*. As much as I've read and studied about the Old West, the program was still a learning experience for me. I was astounded that the program included a female Deputy U.S. Marshal that actually rode the Indian Territory and arrested lawbreakers. I have since researched this elusive person, but have found by archived newspaper articles only that she was very successful in her endeavors.

In my attempt to write as much authenticity as possible into this novel, I visited several entities concerned with U.S. Marshals of the Old West. I give my sincere appreciation to all whom I met and responded to my questions. The sites that I visited are as follows:

> The Fort Smith National Historic Site and Heritage Center, Fort Smith, Arkansas
> The Fort Smith Museum of History, Fort Smith, Arkansas
> The U.S. Marshals Museum Administrative Office, Fort Smith, Arkansas
> Lamar County Historical Museum, Paris, Texas
> Lamar County Historical Society, Paris, Texas
> Chamber of Commerce, Paris, Texas
> Town Square, Paris, Texas
> Oklahoma Territorial Museum, Guthrie, Oklahoma
> Robber's Cave State Park, Oklahoma
> Choctaw Nation Museum, Tuskahoma, Oklahoma

My sincere appreciation goes to Melvin and Nora Bates for taking my wife and me on a day trip to visit Robber's Cave. Their high interest in my project and their knowledge of the history of Oklahoma has contributed immensely to my writing of this novel.

Many thanks to Robert Pulse for providing me information on various research sites concerned with U.S. Marshals and the history of Oklahoma.

Much appreciation goes to my dear friend of many years, Monti Eastin, for her assistance in previewing excerpts of this novel. Her exceptional knowledge in training horses is readily apparent.

Once again, sincere gratitude goes to Gay Lynn Auld for her time, patience, and effort in editing this manuscript. Her suggestions for improvement proved invaluable to the completion of this most intriguing project.

Special thanks to Linda Glover, without whose review and moral support, this book would not have been published.

A very special thanks to my dedicated fans who continue to read my books and consistently ask "When is the next book coming?"

U.S. Marshal Quotation:

"Of all the duties in this country, that of U. S. Marshal is the most dangerous and onerous. The people of the neighboring counties seem to have the idea that the chief use of any officer of the law is to afford a target for their rifles and pistols, and we too well know how many United States officers have fallen victims to duty."

—Springfield, Missouri, Advertiser, May 1876

"Lady Wears a Star"

I humbly dedicate this historical
novel of the Old West to all
female United States Marshals that ever
were, are, or will be in the future.

CHAPTER ONE

A PARTING OF FRIENDS

It was the last day of classes that marked the beginning of summer vacation for the school on the West side of 1880 Paris, Texas. The students in Emily Pritchard's class could hardly contain themselves as the clock on the wall above the blackboard ticked down the final minutes until she would ring the bell for silence and wish all her students a wonderful summer before dismissing them.

Finally, the moment came. All eyes were on Miss Pritchard as she rose from her desk at the front of the class and reached for the hand bell. She hesitated a long moment, watching the children's eyes and smiling widely. She nodded a bit, and then rang the bell signaling summer vacation.

Her students rose almost as one, gathered up their belongings, and turned toward the door where Emily waited to express farewell to each student.

Two best friends, Lydia Forsyth and Annie Schuler, met for a few minutes at a bench in the schoolyard. Annie excitedly announced that her parents, brother, and she would be traveling by wagon to Sherman, Texas to visit with her Aunt Josephine for two weeks before returning to Paris where her father worked his watch and jewelry shop.

Annie quickly cried out, "The trip to Sherman will be near sixty-five miles and take us about three days by our wagon and team. We'll leave early tomorrow morning. We plan to camp out and picnic along the way.

I just know that it will be a fun trip. Aunt Josie is my favorite aunt." As a second thought, Annie smiled and related, "It'll be fun to visit with my cousins also. I'd even bet that there will be a party for us or two."

Lydia voiced her happiness for Annie, "How wonderful for you. It sounds like you'll have a beautiful vacation with your aunt and cousins. I, of course, must stay here in Paris with my mother and father. Father may have to do his business visits to the Indian Territory before long, and I need to help Mother while he is traveling."

It was then, that the two eleven-year-old friends exchanged their small gifts. The two girls fairly ripped open the small packages to gaze with widened eyes at the gift that each had selected for her friend.

As only dear friends might do, they had selected identical matching lockets on gold chains. Each locket held a secret compartment that opened only with the imagination and knowledge of a young girl. Inside each locket was a small portrait of the giver for her friend.

Annie took a deep breath and with eager voice asked her friend Lydia, "Fasten the chain around my neck. I'll do yours."

Lydia complied, and then, turned to have Annie fasten the chain around her neck. The girls took a long moment to gaze at the lockets, their matching gifts of friendship.

"They're beautiful!" breathed Lydia. Annie nodded with a broad smile. Lydia and Annie embraced. As they parted, Lydia spoke first, "I'll keep this locket and your picture forever. You are my best friend." Annie smiled and repeated a similar phrase to Lydia.

Shortly, Annie's mother Edith along with her older brother arrived in their buckboard, their team was a matched pair of strong bay horses that anyone would love to own. The girls exchanged one final hug and then Annie turned to her ride home. Climbing into the back of the two-seater buckboard, she waved farewell to Lydia as her mother turned the wagon toward their home.

Lydia continued to wave as she watched her friend ride off. Loneliness surprisingly enveloped Lydia as her friend disappeared into the distance, but she didn't know why. Lydia turned, walking in an easterly direction, the short distance from town to her home.

2

The next morning after breakfast, the Schuler family loaded their wagon and after all climbed aboard, Jacob Schuler clucked to his team of matched bays, guiding them forward to Sherman.

The family made light chatter as they rode along, talking of the impending two weeks of visiting family. They wondered what activities Aunt Josephine had planned.

Toward dusk, Jacob Schuler surmised they had traveled close to twenty miles. He decided to pull off the dusty road and make their camp for the night. He spoke to his family, "Edith, you and Annie fix our supper. Come on Henri, we'll see to the horses."

After their supper, the family sat around the small campfire speaking in low tones. They talked excitedly about their upcoming visit and about what they might expect on the next day's journey.

A short time later, the family heard the sound of horses approaching from the brushy side of their camp. Within minutes, a gravelly voice rang out of the darkness, "Hallow the camp!"

Without waiting for an answer, three men rode up to the edge of their camp and dismounted. They moved closer into the firelight. The leader spoke, "Saw your campfire in the darkness. We thought you might have a cup of coffee to spare."

The rough looking, unkempt men had eyes that darted all around the camp, taking in the family, the wagon, and the team of matched bays.

Edith and the children moved back a bit from the fire. They held apprehensive looks on their faces.

After long moments, the oldest of the three men who appeared to be the leader spoke again, "We're headed for Garret's Bluff and the ferry. How far would you say that it is?"

Jacob Schuler felt uneasy, but answered, "I believe that it lies north of here, maybe five or six miles."

The man nodded slowly, drew his pistol and then announced, "You look prosperous. We want your valuables, and then we'll leave."

One of the younger men grinned wildly, and mumbled almost coherently, "Yah, and your horses too."

The other young man stared lustily at Edith Schuler and spoke his mind, "That's a good looking woman you got there, mister."

Jacob Schuler could not contain his anger at the young man's offensive comment, "You watch your tongue there young man."

The man scowled at Jacob and again commented, "Yah, mister, that's a fine looking woman you have. I like her. I like her a lot. Wouldn't you say she is a handsome woman sitting there, Gabe?"

"Gabe", the oldest of the three strangers jerked his head around to stare at the young man. He exhaled a long breath and stated, as though resigned to what had to happen next, "Now you've done it. You imbecile, you mentioned my name. There's only one thing to do now."

In the next instant, three revolvers spoke as one. Jacob, Henri, and Annie died instantly.

Edith Schuler jumped up and ran to her husband screaming, "Oh God! Jacob! Henri! Annie! Oh God! My family! My children!"

Horses shied and reared at their hitches, trying to tear loose and gallop away, but Gabe grabbed the reins and steadied them. He admired this pair of bays.

Deke Muller and Josh Kravan both grabbed the woman. Deke slapped her hard across the face to watch her expression suddenly realize what they had in mind for her. She shrieked out, "No! No! Not that!"

The two men dragged Edith into the brush, ripping and tearing her clothes from her. There, they stripped her naked and ravaged her as they saw fit.

Edith's screams went unheeded by the elements of nature.

Gabe, having settled the animals, rummaged the bodies of the murdered man and his children. He found Jacob's money belt strapped around his waist inside his shirt and he looked quickly over his shoulder to insure that the other two men had not seen him take it.

He quickly counted the money. Jacob had been carrying well over a thousand dollars in currency. He deliberately took most of the money and stashed it in his saddlebags. He then took Jacob's rings and gold watch.

The boy had nothing of value on his person. He glanced down at the girl whose eyes were wide with the horror of a savage death. Something glinted around her neck. He bent down closer to her.

It was a gold chain and locket. He liked it. He reached down and savagely tore it from around her neck. He held the locket up to his eyes and it glimmered in the glare of the fire. He thought to himself, "A nice watch fob for me."

Momentarily, another shot rang out and Gabe knew that the two men had finished their ravage and ended the woman's life.

Within a few minutes, both stepped into the light of the campfire. They looked around and knew that Gabe had secured the valuables.

Gabe smiled at them, "Boys, we got three hundred dollars to split between us. In addition, you two can take the team of horses. We'll leave that wagon behind. It would be too noticeable for us. All right, let's get mounted and make for that ferry. I expect to be in the Indian Territory by daybreak. Once there, no law can track us."

Dawn found the three murderers at Garrett's Ferry, anxious to cross. Jesse Garrett looked appraisingly at two of the three rough-dressed, distasteful men. The third man who appeared somewhat older kept himself turned away from Jesse's gaze and he couldn't say for certain what the man looked like.

Jesse felt that he needed to get shunt of this bunch as soon as he could. He nodded affirmatively to the men, "It's earlier than usual, but I'll take you across. That'll be three dollars for the three of you and your stock."

One of the younger men paid the fare and after loading the ferry, Jesse struck out across the Red River to land on the edge of the Indian Territory, most notably, on the land of the Choctaw Nation.

When, the men disembarked on the Indian Territory side, they mounted and rode off toward the north trailing the stolen bays. Garrett breathed easier then. He didn't like the looks or mannerisms of any of the three men. He shrugged and started his ferry back across the river to the Texas side.

CHAPTER TWO

A GRIM DISCOVERY

Mid-morning the following day, a mounted Silas Miller lead his two-wagon freighting outfit along the trail from Paris toward Sherman. As they approached a small clearing along the trail, Silas' horse suddenly alerted and stepped to the side of the road.

At the same time, the mules pulling the lead wagon balked and headed toward the edge of the road.

Silas reined his animal in hard as he took careful note of the trail ahead. He hadn't noticed until this moment that the sky ahead was filled with the dark birds of prey—vultures.

Silas raised his arm in the signal to halt the wagons. Turning in the saddle, he called out to his lead teamster, "Buster! Hold the wagons here. I'm going forward. Keep your weapons at the ready, just in case."

Silas urged his mount ahead at a walk, his eyes scanning the terrain for movement or some clue as to what worried his animals.

A hundred yards further and Silas exhaled an audible, "Holy Mother of God!" His eyes took in the horrible scene just off the road.

A lone two-seat wagon stood amongst a litter-strewn landscape. A travel trunk and valise were smashed on the ground with contents scattered all over the ground. Family clothing rippled in the slight breeze. An overturned picnic basket lay covered with ants all over fresh meats and bread.

It was then that Silas saw the broken bodies of a man, boy, and young girl. Their clothes were ripped open as if the perpetrators were searching for valuables hidden on them. The scene caused the old man to feel sick to his stomach.

Moving closer, he recognized Jacob Schuler. With heart pounding in his chest, he scanned the brush along the edge of the grisly scene. There he found Edith without her clothes and a bullet between her eyes. He felt certain that she had been violated before the gunshot pierced her skull. The look of her final minutes forever etched on her swollen face.

Silas ran back to the road frantically waving his teamsters forward. He looked back at the scene, his mind racing—to decide what he should do.

Where was the nearest lawman? Should he bury the hapless family here?

Respect for the wife of his friend brought Silas to survey the scene once more to secure something to cover her ravaged and mutilated body. Seeing the picnic blanket, he quickly gathered it up and covered poor Edith's body.

He then picked up articles of clothing to cover the faces of Mr. Schuler and his children.

The freight wagons drew up and the four men riding the high wagon seats could view the carnage. They slowly climbed down from their wagons with hesitation, questioning looks on each of their faces.

"What are we to do?" queried Buster, the chief teamster, pulling his sleeve across his face to wipe his face and hide his tears.

Silas removed his black weather-beaten slouch hat and mopped his forehead with his bandana while searching for a reply. His eyes darted from the deceased family to the circling vultures. He replaced his hat and stroked his whiskers for another long moment. At last, he made a decision.

"There's got to be some sort of law at Garrett's Bluff. That's about five to six miles from here at the river. Buster, you and the men camp here and guard this scene. Don't let no curious travelers rummage this area or stand around gawking at the scene, should any come riding along this road. And—you keep them devil birds from them dead folks. I'm going to Garrett's to bring back whatever law I can find there. I should be back within a couple of hours."

Silas searched the eyes of his teamsters. They nodded in agreement.

The old man mounted and urgently spurred his mount toward Garrett's Bluff.

Two hours later, Silas rode up to the ferry and inquired of Jesse Garrett, "Garrett, is there a lawman at this place? I have urgent need of the law."

Jesse saw the strained look on the man's face and replied, "Not usually, but today you're in luck. There are two Texas Rangers having noon meal in my waiting room. What's this about anyway?"

The old freighting master cleared his throat and quickly related to Jesse, "There's been murder and robbery. Better yet, I'd call it the massacre and desecration of a family."

Jesse closed his eyes for a moment as he recalled the three men who had crossed the Red River early that morning. He replied, "I'll come with you and point out the Rangers."

Silas dismounted, and then the two men walked the short distance to the passenger waiting area in Jesse's cabin.

Jesse led Silas to the dining table where two men sat eating their noon meal and drinking coffee. There, after handshakes all around, Silas informed Rangers John Beckham and Jim Strahan of his discovery.

"Me and my freighting outfit were on the Sherman Road just south of here when we saw a lot of vultures circling. I went forward to see what unlucky critter they was getting set to feast on. That's when I found them. A man, well dressed and two children, a boy of teen age and a young girl. They'd been shot to death. A further look around and we found the woman. She'd been stripped of her clothes, and defiled before they done her in."

Silas swallowed hard before continuing, "Their wagon was empty of animals, with their harnesses lying on the ground. The wagon is of good make. The family's belongings were dumped on the ground and scattered all around, like the culprits rummaged for valuables before making off with the team."

It was then that Jesse added, "And, I think those that done it crossed into the Nations early this morning. There were three rough-dressed men that acted mighty peculiar. They had a pair of bay horses with them that seemed way too good for the likes of them fellers."

Jesse continued, "The two younger ones were both tall and unshaven. One was blonde and the other sort of red haired. The blonde one held a wicked gleam in his eyes. The older hombre was very trail savvy. He kept his hat brim pulled down low on his face, so I couldn't make out his features too well. In fact, most of the time in the ferry, he kept his back to my gaze. The two young ones referred to him as "Gabe." I was sure glad to get clear of them on the other side of the river."

The Rangers listened intently to what Jesse Garret related. Then, Ranger Beckham turned to his partner, "Jim, we'd better go with this man and see what goes."

He looked at Silas, "Give us a few minutes to get our mounts saddled, and then, you can guide us to this murder scene, Mr. Miller." Silas acknowledged with a nod of his head.

An hour or so later, Silas and the Rangers arrived at the grisly scene. Silas answered questions about the scene before his freighters moved into the campsite. He mentioned that by the tracks around the site, there were at least three outlaws involved and that the tracks of five horses led off in the direction of the Garret's Bluff ferry.

After Ranger Beckham had thoroughly checked the area and taken down some notes, he turned to the freighting foreman, "Mr. Miller, we'd like for you and your men to bury the family here together because of the extreme summer heat. Ranger Strahan and I will travel on to Paris and notify the sheriff of this travesty. We will tell the sheriff that we left the family buried and their wagon as is. Please pick up all the family's belongings and place them back in their luggage. Leave them on the wagon. I feel sure that there will be a posse out here by tomorrow afternoon, along with the undertaker to reclaim the dead and take them home."

Ranger Beckham stood deep in thought for a long moment before he again addressed Silas and his freighters.

"It's a sad state of affairs, but Texas Rangers are not allowed to enter the Indian Territory. We sure would like to track these scavengers down and get justice for these hapless folks. We will get word to the Sheriff at Paris about this outrage and the location. Mr. Miller, after these people are buried, you and your men can continue on your journey. Thank you, men. Thank you for being good citizens."

Silas and his men were dumbfounded. Silas shook his head attempting to make sense of this. "What are you saying Ranger Beckham? What do you mean you can't go into the Territory after that scum that did this?"

Ranger Beckham recounted his statement, "That's correct Silas. Texas Rangers cannot enter the Territory to arrest anyone. Only a United States Marshal can enter the Nations and arrest lawbreakers. The sheriff at Paris will have to notify Judge Parker at Fort Smith for warrants. He holds jurisdiction over the entire Indian Territory."

Beckham waited a moment, "We will advise the sheriff. He will know what to do."

CHAPTER THREE

A HARD DECISION

Jonathan Forsyth was the mercantile agent for a company headquartered in Dallas, Texas. While he routinely traveled each month throughout his assigned region of North Texas and the Choctaw Nation to secure orders for restock of the company's products, this final week of the month found him in town to process orders.

At midday, Jonathan was talking with a prospective client over lunch when Sheriff Barnes burst into the café seeking the undertaker. Jonathan caught bits of the subdued conversation. With this news, his heart pounded like a locomotive against his chest. His ears heard only muffled conversation after the first few sentences. He felt like he was suddenly deaf.

He had understood enough of the conversation to know that the Schuler family had been found dead on the road to Sherman. When the lawman and undertaker left, Forsyth quickly excused himself to follow the sheriff and undertaker out of the café.

"Sheriff Barnes!" the distraught man shouted.

Bob Barnes turned quickly to see who hailed him. "What do you want, Forsyth? I have an urgent matter to tend to."

Forsyth cried out, "I caught the drift of your notice to Undertaker Brothers. Can this be true? Has the Schuler family been murdered?"

Sheriff Barnes swallowed the tight lump in his throat before answering his friend. "Forsyth, this ain't the time to discuss details of a sheriff's case.

But, I know how close your daughter Lydia is to the Shuler girl. I will tell you that two Texas Rangers left here minutes ago on their way to Dallas. They informed me of a crime scene that they witnessed earlier today. They related that four members of the Schuler family were found dead. Yes, Annie Schuler was among them. I just don't know how I am going to tell my girl, Emily. Emily and the Schuler girl were friends also."

Bob Barnes hung his head for a long moment before speaking once again, "Mr. Brothers and his people will accompany me and a small posse in the morning to the site. We'll retrieve the bodies to return them home to Paris. That's what I can tell you right now, Forsyth."

Jonathan stared at the sheriff. He was without words. His body trembled. In disbelief, he turned away from Barnes and walked with unsteady gait back to the restaurant to bid good day to his client.

Heartbroken, the father immediately pondered how he would break this news to Lydia. It was a dreaded task that he must do. He contemplated the times. This was 1880 and the country was wild. Geronimo continued to wreck havoc throughout the Southwest, the army in constant pursuit. The James gang was hunted, and Jonathan's business route in the Indian Territory was refuge for many a man hunted by the law.

Jonathan continued to reflect on his travels in the Territory, where he visited various trading posts to promote the wares of his company. On these journeys, he made his way sufficiently armed with shotgun and revolving pistol.

On occasion, he encountered unsavory characters in his travel, thus he envisioned those who came upon the Schuler family, killing each in cold blood for their money, animals, and personal effects. Jonathan surmised that there were those at hand near Paris, Texas capable of such travesty.

Arriving home earlier than usual, Jonathan stabled his horse and stripped it of saddle and gear. As he took care of his animal, the worried man mulled over words to relate the Schuler family's demise to Laura and especially to his daughter, Lydia.

He knew what he had to do. Anxiety gripped the man as he slowly moved toward the house. As he approached his wife and daughter, he was met with, "Jonathan! You're home early. Is there something wrong?"

Jonathan stopped short of his wife and daughter. The two turned from the laundry to face him. With ashen face, he attempted to force a smile as he responded, "Yes, Laura. I need to speak with you alone briefly. Lydia, please excuse us while we discuss something of importance."

Lydia was concerned, but obeyed her father. "I'll be in my room, Father."

Laura looked with alarm and saw the pain in Jonathan's eyes. His mind had churned for what seemed like an eternity.

"What is it, Jonathan? What distresses you so that it brought you home this early?

"Laura," he replied, "the Schuler family has been found dead on the road to Sherman."

Laura's eyes widened with shock and her hands came up to her face.

Jonathan continued, "Texas Rangers apprised Sheriff Barnes of it only hours ago. It seems the marauders have crossed the Red River into the Indian Territory. The Rangers are forbidden to enter the Nations and could not follow them. We must tell Lydia. I simply don't know how to do it myself."

Laura and Jonathan's eyes met. Tears flowed down her cheeks as she stammered, "Oh Lord! I can't believe this world. We must both go to Lydia and talk to her. We must relate that sometimes, good people are in the wrong place at the wrong time. We'll tell her how bad people take advantage of folks, stealing their belongings. She is of the age to know that danger lies about us."

Laura continued, "Yes, Jonathan, we must both be there when you tell her. To be together as a family is paramount when bad news is announced. Lydia will be devastated, but she is strong. Time will heal her broken heart. Trust me, Jonathan. She is a strong young lady."

Laura and Jonathan walked hand in hand to Lydia's room. Her father rapped on the door. Lydia responded quickly, opening the door with a perplexed look at her parents.

"May we come in?" said Laura, her voice faint.

"Yes, come in, both of you. What is it, Mother? What is it, Father?"

"Please, we must all sit together," said her mother with emotion. Jonathan and Laura sat on either side of Lydia on her bed. "There is something that you must know. It concerns your friend Annie Schuler and her family. Let's let Father speak."

"Lydia," began Jonathan, "You know the country here in the West remains wild and dangerous, despite movements for law and order. There's been many social improvements. But, sometimes," Jonathan choked on his words. "lonely roads far from town provide men with evil hearts the opportunity to take advantage of good weary travelers. Something has happened to our friends, the Schuler family."

Lydia's eyes went wide and her mouth slacked. She gripped and squeezed her mother's hands.

Jonathan swallowed hard before continuing, "My heart aches that I must tell you that your friend Annie and her family were murdered on the road to Sherman. Sheriff Barnes gave me notice earlier that Texas Rangers stopped in at his office to let him know. The sheriff with a posse along with Mr. Brothers, our undertaker, and his men will go tomorrow to bring the Schuler family back to Paris for a proper burial."

Lydia cried out, "Oh My God! My best friend, Annie has been— murdered? Please tell me that this is not true! Not my friend Annie!"

Lydia's knees gave way and she fell into a heap onto her Mother. Jonathan reached out to Lydia. She withdrew, her eyes wide in disbelief. "No! I refuse to believe it! No, this did not happen!"

Lydia bolted from her room and out the front door of their home. Jonathan stood up to stop his daughter. Laura touched his arm and whispered, "Let her go, Jonathan. She will return soon."

Adrenaline rushed as Lydia raced like a deer in the woods to their special meeting place in the schoolyard. The girl slumped on a wooden bench, cradling her face on the rough table. Only yesterday, Annie sat across from Lydia to share word of her family journey to begin soon.

She reached to her throat and clutched the locket, a gift from Annie. She closed her eyes and tried to envision Annie. Suddenly, she gasped. A vision of Annie appeared in her mind and Lydia clutched the pendant at her neck more closely. "Annie doesn't have her locket anymore."

Lydia's heart thumped wildly as the realization of what had happened. Grief enveloped her very being.

Several minutes passed as Lydia held her pose. Finally, she whispered the words that would enshrine her friend forever. "Annie, you will always be my friend. Although you are gone from my sight, you will always be in my heart."

An hour passed before Lydia stood up from the table with an aura of resolve. She had made a decision and now wanted to speak frankly with her father and mother. The child, mature beyond her years, walked slowly back to her home and entered.

Laura and Jonathan sat together in the kitchen. They looked up from their coffee to see Lydia's tear streaked, stricken face.

"Mother, Father. Please hold me." Jonathan held out his arms to his child who moved into the shelter of her father's grasp. Laura joined the pair, bringing the Forsyth family encircled in close embrace. There were no words to express their grief.

Lydia spoke first, "Father, starting tomorrow, I want you to teach me the gun. I want to know how and when to use a pistol." Her assertiveness startled Jonathan. He looked into the pleading eyes of his daughter. How should he respond? He looked to Laura, realizing she had read his thoughts.

Jonathan saw fear and grief in his wife's eyes. Their young daughter had experienced the trauma of losing her best friend at the hand of violence. A portion of her sweet innocence had been torn from Lydia. As a Mother, Laura longed to keep her young daughter just that; a girl who learned to bake fruit pies, and who longed for nothing more than a new Sunday dress.

Laura pondered her thoughts for several minutes before speaking, "Jonathan. I believe that Lydia has a great need just now. Although I would prefer otherwise, I must agree with her. After all, it was you, who taught me to shoot when we first came to Texas. Yes, Jonathan, teach Lydia in the same manner that you taught me. Teach her all about the why, when to use, how to use, and care of your revolver."

Laura paused in reflection for a moment, "In fact, after I learned the gun from you, you bought me my own revolver, one that fits easily in my hand. I now believe that Lydia is a responsible young woman and I am sure that she will heed your lessons and words of caution."

Jonathan was awestruck that Laura would consent to Lydia learning to shoot and care for a weapon. He nodded his head. He knew other men in town who had already taught their young sons. In fact, Sheriff Bob Barnes spoke recently of teaching his son James to shoot. He thought, "Why would teaching a daughter be any different? My mind would rest more easily knowing my daughter could defend herself. Yes, it is a good idea."

Jonathan was certain he should inquire where Sheriff Barnes took his son on the edge of Paris for instruction in the use of firearms.

"All right dear," replied Jonathan, "we will start your revolver instruction on this next Saturday afternoon, after I consult Sheriff Barnes."

Thus, it began. Lydia Forsyth would become expert in handling a revolver. Little did she nor anyone else realize the impact of these lessons on Lydia's future.

CHAPTER FOUR

JUSTICE FINDS THE GUILTY

Late the following afternoon, a somber procession led by Sheriff Barnes and six posse members on horseback arrived at the city of Paris, Texas. With them were Mr. Brothers, the undertaker, and his funeral attendants. The four gravediggers rode atop a large freight wagon pulled by a team of four sturdy mules. Four makeshift coffins lay strapped to the bed of the wagon.

The Schuler's personal dual seated wagon, loaded with the family baggage along with other trappings was double-hitched to the burial freight wagon.

Residents of Paris stood in silence as the grim procession passed the square. Men removed their hats out of respect while the women folk pulled handkerchiefs from their blouse sleeves as they wept. Word of the Schuler family murder had spread through the city of Paris, Texas.

Those who knew the Schuler family wept openly. As townspeople watched the grim parade, most wondered when justice would come for this grisly outrage.

Lydia Forsyth and her parents stood amongst the citizens who lined the Paris town square when the solemn column moved slowly towards the funeral parlor. The girl held her mother's hand tightly. Tears openly flowed down her cheeks. In her mind's eye, Lydia recreated Annie at the last moment when they parted at the schoolyard several days earlier. Now, it seemed forever ago to the distraught girl.

The cavalcade arrived at the mortuary yard, moving through the gates to the receiving area at the rear of the building. The gates were closed behind the entourage until once again they opened momentarily. Two grim faced deputies with rifles cradled in their arms appeared and took up a guardian stance just outside the gate.

Onlookers moved toward the undertaker's courtyard and stood silently meditating the situation. They looked for answers about the rumored massacre of a well-known and respected Paris, Texas family.

Minutes ticked by before Sheriff Barnes with his posse exited the funeral home front entrance. Two deputies carried wooden straight back chairs from inside and took up vigilance on both sides of the door. Each held his rifle across his lap.

Meanwhile, Sheriff Barnes stepped off the wooden boardwalk to face the gathering mourners. Barnes swallowed hard before speaking in an authoritative voice, "People of Paris! The Schuler family is home to rest. It was a despicable act. We will work to insure that those responsible are made to pay for this heinous crime. A warrant request will be dispatched to Judge Parker at Fort Smith. I am confident that he will issue warrants to his U.S. Marshals with jurisdiction in the Indian Territory to find and arrest those who are guilty."

He waited a moment to allow the crowd to ponder his words. He continued, "Please return to your business now and allow Mr. Brothers to perform his duty. There is nothing more to witness. The date and time of the funerals will be posted at my office and obituaries printed in the newspapers."

Friends of the Schuler family remained for several minutes in quiet reflection, some in hushed intimate conversation before taking leave of the mortuary.

The Forsyth family walked in silence to their home for the evening. The following morning, Jonathan would speak to Sheriff Barnes regarding firearm training for Lydia.

Early the next morning Jonathan stepped into the Paris jail and, encountering Deputy Sheriff Bradford, inquired, "Hello, George. Is Bob Barnes around?"

George Bradford replied, "Sheriff Barnes is over at Miller's Café for his breakfast. Might I help you with something?"

Jonathan smiled, "No, George. It's a private matter. I'll walk over to the café to speak to Bob. Thanks for the information." George nodded his understanding.

Jonathan left the jail walking briskly to the café. Inside, he found Bob Barnes hunkered down over a breakfast of eggs, ham, fried potatoes, and thick sliced tomato. A large cup of hot coffee sat near his right hand.

Maude Miller, the owner of the small café, observed Jonathan enter her establishment and moved across the room to greet him. "Good Morning, Jonathan. What brings you to my small place? You usually go elsewhere for breakfast."

Jonathan smiled at Maude, "Yes, Maude, I do usually breakfast at home or down at the square, but today I need to speak to Bob Barnes. I'll enjoy a cup of your coffee, if you please."

Maude moved behind the counter to fill his request while Jonathan stepped up to Bob's table, "Good morning, Bob. I have a delicate question for you, and I thought that we should speak alone. I've ordered coffee. May I sit down?"

Sheriff Barnes nodded his agreement and Jonathan slid into a chair across from his friend. Their eyes met and held for a long minute. No words were exchanged. Maude brought Jonathan's coffee and when Bob Barnes finished his last bite, they moved to a less conspicuous table near the wall, bringing their coffee.

The two men remained silent until Maude moved out of earshot. Jonathan nervously cleared his voice before speaking. "Sheriff, I understand that you are currently teaching your son James the gun. I understand that you are instructing him on the how, when, and wherefores of shooting a weapon. Is that true?"

Bob Barnes glanced carefully around the room before replying. "Yes, Jonathan, that is true. James is going on twelve now and I feel that every young boy should be taught weapons use and care responsibly by their fathers. My father taught me and I trust that your father taught you. That's the way of it. Let's face it, Jonathan, any place west of the Mississippi is still frontier. Sad but true, being this close to the Territory, one can never know what to expect anymore."

Jonathan closed his eyes for a long moment before commenting further. Bob wondered about the question since Jonathan didn't have sons. When he again faced Barnes, he stated his case bluntly. "Bob, I want to instruct Lydia on the use and care of firearms for her safety. I would like us to join you and James for your lessons. Where do you conduct your shooting training? Would you consider us joining you?"

Sheriff Barnes looked directly at his friend. He saw the need. He pondered his reply for a moment. "Jonathan, I've not known of teaching a young girl how to shoot around here, but if you've a mind to, and you think it needed, then James and I would welcome you and Lydia when we practice. We start usually around eight o'clock in the morning and ride out to the bluffs along the river. We set up some targets and take our time practicing aim, shooting technique, and care of our weapons."

Barnes hesitated a moment in thought, "Does Lydia have her own gun yet? I had to buy James his own revolver since he is still too young to carry and properly handle a Colt .44 Revolver. Check with Bjorne Almquist at his gun shop. He helped me with a small caliber revolver for James. I'm sure that he could fit Lydia with one of her own."

Jonathan finished his coffee and thanked the Sheriff for his time and invitation. He left the café, heading directly to the town gunsmith shop.

A bell rang as Jonathan Forsyth entered Almquist's Gun Shop. He glanced around the one room store. Bjorne sat in the rear of the shop bent over a work desk that held a Colt Frontier frame in a vice.

The elderly gentleman was tinkering with the mechanism. Bjorne looked up at him over his wire-rimmed spectacles and smiled. "Good day to you, Sir. Vat can I do for you today?"

Jonathan returned pleasantries and responded, "I need a gun for a young lady who wishes to learn how to shoot. Do you have such a small gun?"

Bjorne thought for a moment, then replied, "Jah! I think I haf just the right gun for a young lady."

Mr. Almquist rose from his workbench and moved to a cabinet behind a front counter. He opened it and after studying for a minute or two, he selected and withdrew a small .32 caliber revolving pistol with bone grips. He presented it to Jonathan.

Jonathan studied the size and weight of the revolver, thinking of Lydia's hands, and asked, "Where did you get this weapon?"

Bjorne grinned as he related, "Vel, dis pistol vas traded to me by a young lady gambler. She was quite the lady, but very lethal to cheaters. She decided that she needed something with more stopping power after she had to shoot an angry card player three times to lay him out."

Bjorne chuckled a bit after that, as Jonathan's eyes widened in wonder. He'd never tell Laura or Lydia <u>that</u> account of this revolver.

When Jonathan recovered a bit from Bjorne's comments, he continued, "How much do you want for this piece?"

Bjorne pondered Jonathan's question and after a moment, replied, "Would this piece be for the young Lydia?"

Jonathan was taken back at the gunsmith's question but managed to stammer, "Why, yes! It is. Why do you ask?"

The elderly gunsmith answered, "I haf heard about the Schuler family. I know of the friendship between Annie Schuler and your daughter Lydia. My son Joseph told me. I also saw the family coffins brought back to town by Sheriff Barnes and his posse. I will sell this gun to you for Lydia for only five dollars although it is worth much more. I understand why she wants to learn and this is a good start for her."

With a humble thank you, Jonathan purchased the revolver, along with a box of .32 caliber ammunition for his daughter to practice using the firearm.

In the days following, Sheriff Barnes was good on his word. A wanted notice was dispatched to Judge Issac Parker at Fort Smith. The Judge immediately issued a warrant for the arrest of the three murderers and dispatched it with his party of U.S. Marshals into the Indian Territory.

In the meantime, Jonathan and Lydia joined Sherriff Barnes and his son every weekend at an isolated spot along the Red River. They practiced weapon use and safety along with an hour or so of live target practice. Both Lydia and James became familiar with their very own revolvers.

Two months after Judge Parker issued the murder warrant, his U.S.

Marshals had a stroke of luck when they found the Schuler wagon team animals. The man who held them advised that he had purchased the animals from two young men. He provided descriptions of each and relayed their possible whereabouts.

Only a few days later Deke Muller and Josh Kraven, were surprised at their campsite located deep into the Choctaw Nation by Deputy Marshals, who arrested them without incident.

The outlaws were escorted to the federal jail at Fort Smith, Arkansas, and held for trial.

Fort Smith newspapers reported that each man accused the other of murdering the woman. The two outlaws yelled and screamed at each other during their trial calling each other liars. Obscenities, name calling, and accusations consistently interrupted the trial.

Each denied killing any others of the family relating that their leader, *Gabe*, did the rest of the family in. They described the older man *Gabe* to the court but could not give his whereabouts.

Several days later Judge Parker sentenced both men to hang for the violation and murder of Edith Schuler and the theft of the Schuler family wagon team, as well as being accomplices to the murder of the other family members.

The last words from both men before justice was carried out by the Fort Smith hangman remained, *"Gabe did it."*

A weekly newspaper, *The Fort Smith Elevator,* carried the full story of the arrest, trial, and hanging of the two men. Copies of the paper arrived in Paris, Texas within the week and were immediately sold out, and then passed hand-to-hand as the community read of the justice administered by Judge Parker at the Fort Smith Circuit Court.

CHAPTER FIVE

STRANGE LADY IN TOWN

January 1, 1890 ushered in the era that would later be termed, "The Gay Nineties." Major European cities were alive with antics of the rich and famous, who took to parties, socials, and major fashion changes. Such was the same in major American cities. New York boasted of socialites attending lavish parties. New music seemed the staple of the East. The face of dancing changed dramatically, and cities east of Chicago swung into the fervor of the era.

West of the Mississippi, however, the land remained unchanged by the fervor of the East in its gaiety. Geronimo and his Apache renegades were still wrecking havoc throughout the Southwest, and the city of Paris, Texas still sat on the edge of one of the most dangerous territories of the West.

The Indian Territory jurisdiction was now divided into three separate entities. Fort Leavenworth, Kansas held jurisdiction for the northern territory; Fort Smith, Arkansas and Judge Isaac Parker still held jurisdiction for the center of the Territory, and Paris, Texas now held the newly assigned jurisdiction for the Southern Indian Territory, namely, the Choctaw and Chickasaw Nations. The Indian Territory was often referred to as The Territory, The Nations, and more specifically by the tribe's names, such as The Choctaw Nation, The Chickasaw Nation, or The Cherokee Nation.

It was mid-June when the train from points south slowly chugged into the station at Paris, Texas. Nate Brown, one of the station's porters, hurried to the passenger cars in order to assist arriving passengers with their luggage. He reached the second car and stood beside the rear steps anxious to assist with any requests.

He glanced up to observe a dark haired young woman attired in maroon skirt and matching waist jacket and white blouse adorned with a ruby broach emerge from the rear entrance of the car. Nate held his hand up to help her dismount the rail car. She carried a carpetbag that seemed fairly well packed.

The lady was tall, perhaps five foot seven, and of slender build. She smiled at Nate when he reached up to take her hand and help her step down to the wooden platform of the station house. Nate noticed her eyes. They were hazel and seemed to sparkle with a vitality for life.

Nate held out his other hand to take hold of the carpetbag and then he walked with the young woman toward the station. At the baggage car, they hesitated just long enough for her to point out her trunk, which had been checked to Paris. She requested that he insure its delivery to the front of the station where horse taxi service waited for possible customers that needed transportation into the city.

Lydia Forsyth walked beside the porter through the station house and to the front where the local transportation waited. She motioned to a wooden bench and proceeded to sit down. Nate Brown set the carpetbag next to her and indicated that he would be back directly with her checked trunk.

While she waited, Lydia scanned the area of the rail station as well as the surrounding landscape. It was familiar to her and she smiled a bit. She was home at last after four long years at the Lady's Academy in Dallas, Texas. She had only been back for two special funerals.

Both her mother and her father had passed on, and although she was now alone in the world, she had a burning vision as to what she wanted to do with her life. She would put those plans in motion the very next day, but first, she would visit the cemetery. There were those that lay there that she loved.

Momentarily, Nate returned with her travel trunk and set it down beside her. Lydia smiled up at him and presented him a Morgan silver dollar for his services.

Nate was astounded. Most folks usually tipped him much less, around a quarter of a dollar. He sort of choked up and looked down at Lydia who replied to his questioning glance with "Thank you, Sir. You have provided a great service to me. Now, one more task. Would you please select the best taxi driver for me, one that would take me to wherever I would want to go? I grew up here in Paris and I am familiar with the town and surrounding area."

Nate grinned widely. This lady was polite, but very knowledgeable about people. "Yes, Ma'am. I will do just that. The best taxi driver is Frank Sutton. That's him right over there, near the end of the station house." Nate picked up her travel trunk and started toward the waiting taxi.

"Frank Sutton!" The name sounded familiar to Lydia. Her mind raced as she recalled her early life in Paris. Then, she remembered. Frank Sutton was a classmate of hers at the elementary school. She grinned widely. Frank was known as a friendly fellow, but often a prankster in the sixth grade. He would definitely be surprised at her now.

When she reached the taxi, the driver turned around and stepped forward to take her satchel. A look of surprise crossed his face and he grinned widely. "Lydia Forsyth! I haven't seen you in well over four years. What have you been doing and where did you disappear to?"

Lydia replied, "It's good to be back, Frank. I've been at a ladies school in Dallas for the past four years. I've graduated and now want to make my home here in Paris. This is where I belong."

Frank nodded his understanding, "Welcome home, Lydia. Where would you like to go?"

She responded, "I want to go to the cemetery for a few minutes, first. Then, I'll go on to the Peterson Hotel. I'll get a room there until I can make some more permanent arrangement."

Nate had already placed the trunk into the bed of the taxi and stepped back a bit. Frank acknowledged her request and, taking her satchel, he placed it in the luggage bed of his taxi and helped Lydia up into the cab. Frank climbed up into the driver's seat and clucked to his team of matched bays. Twenty minutes later, they entered the Paris cemetery area and Lydia directed him to the place she wanted to stop.

He helped Lydia step out of the taxi, "Wait here, Frank. I want to pay my respects. I'll be here briefly."

Frank acknowledged with a nod as Lydia stepped down a short path. He decided to take a few minutes break from his taxi service. He walked out of Lydia's sight around to the other side of the taxi, reached into his inside vest pocket and took out one of those new fangled already rolled cigarettes. Striking a sulfur match, he lit it up and took a deep inhale of the tobacco. He pondered Lydia's return to Paris as he enjoyed his cigarette while lazily blowing smoke rings into the air.

A quarter hour passed and Lydia appeared beside the taxi. "Thank you for waiting, Frank. Now, I suppose that I should go and get a room at the Peterson Hotel. As we drive, you can bring me up to date as to the latest happenings here in Paris."

Frank thought that was a nice idea. He helped Lydia back up into the taxi. This time, he asked her to sit beside him as he drove his two-horse hack. On the way to the hotel, Frank apprised Lydia of the new businesses in the area, some stories about some of their classmates from school, and it seemed the most exciting news was the newly assigned Federal District Court of Paris, which now held jurisdiction over the Southern Indian Territory.

Excitement gleamed in Frank's eyes as he told about the large number of Deputy U.S. Marshals in town. He further advised that, "There is a federal courthouse to be built, but for the moment, the Marshals keep temporary office in the Lamar County Courthouse just over on the next block behind the town square."

Now, that was information that Lydia wanted to hear. She would stroll down to the courthouse the very next morning and reveal her reason for returning to Paris.

Momentarily, Frank drew up his taxi team in front of the Peterson Hotel on the square. He jumped down from his driver box and rounded his team to help Lydia to the ground. He then moved to the luggage boot and retrieved Lydia's travel trunk and carpetbag. He set both carefully on the walk.

Lydia opened her handbag and was about to offer Frank payment for the ride. He smiled widely, saying, "This ride is on the house. It is nice seeing you again, Lydia. I hope to see you around town in days forth." She thanked him for his generosity and watched him remount his taxi and drive off back to the rail station.

A porter stepped out to the street from the hotel and carried Lydia's luggage to the registration desk. She followed the porter and stood beside the counter while the clerk concluded his business with the gentleman ahead of her.

At her turn, she registered as Lydia Forsyth of Dallas, Texas. The clerk observed the signature and smiled. He also had attended the school a year behind Lydia. He welcomed her to Paris and inquired as to what floor she would prefer to be boarded on. She pondered only a moment before answering, "The second floor if you please." The clerk turned to his pigeon hole key and mail box for a moment and withdrew a room key.

"Here you are, Miss Forsyth. Room number 214 is yours for as long as you'd like to stay with us." He smiled as he handed her the key. He also waved to the patiently waiting porter to carry her luggage up the stairs to her assigned room.

Once inside the small but quaint room, Lydia had the porter place her travel trunk on a small stand and her valise at the foot of the bed. She reached into her handbag and found an appropriate coin to tip the porter. She shut the door after the porter left and slipped the lock into place.

She looked around the room, taking in the décor and comfort afforded by the room. "Yes," she thought, "this room will do nicely until I can locate a more suitable place to reside in Paris."

Lydia went to the wooden wardrobe standing along the wall and opened it. There was ample space for her hang up clothes. She removed her jacket and hung it up on a wooden hanger. For the next few minutes, she unpacked her travel trunk and hung her dresses, blouses, skirts, and jackets in the wardrobe.

The last item that she removed from her travel trunk was a folded leather gun belt with holster. The belt was custom made for Lydia and its loops were filled with brass cartridges of the .44 caliber. She hung this item on a hook in the wardrobe also.

After closing her travel trunk and storing it in a corner, Lydia moved to the foot of the bed and opened her valise. She reached inside and silently withdrew two revolvers. One revolver was a pocket-sized Colt .41 caliber revolver with walnut grips and a two and one-half inch barrel. The second revolver was a Colt .44 Frontier, her favorite handgun and the one for which her holster was fashioned. She smiled slightly as she held the antler-gripped weapon lightly and balanced it in her right hand.

Lydia moved back to the wardrobe and slipped the Colt Frontier Revolver into the holster. Then, she placed the pocket revolver into her handbag. She would carry it as she surveyed the town square after a meal at the hotel café.

Later that evening, Lydia returned to her room and readied herself for the night. She washed her face and hands in the porcelain basin after pouring water from the matching white pitcher. A lightly fragranced bar of soap, a nice touch, lay handy next to the basin along with a small stack of hand towels.

After changing into a cotton nightgown, she slipped into the bed. It seemed comfortable enough. Then, the newly arrived "Lady from Dallas" turned down the oil lamp on the nightstand next to the bed.

Her mind visualized the plans that she had for the next morning. Satisfied that she was doing the right thing, she closed her eyes and slipped off into a land of easy slumber.

CHAPTER SIX

A NEW STAR FOR JUSTICE

Early the next morning, Lydia emerged from her room at the Peterson Hotel dressed in a plum colored skirt and waist jacket with light beige blouse buttoned at the neck. She carried her handbag in her left hand as she walked to a café just down from the Peterson for a bite of breakfast.

Thoughts whirled through her mind as she partook of sliced ham, two fried eggs, and a small helping of fried potatoes. The coffee was hot, strong, and tasted especially good this morning. Today she would speak to the United States Marshal of the newly created district court for the Southern Indian Territory.

Lydia had read of the need for Deputy U.S. Marshals for this important assignment in the Dallas newspapers, and she had it in mind to be one of them. She was determined to convince the U.S. Marshal in charge of her qualities and capabilities. This lady could handle herself quite well, and was ready to prove her mettle under difficult situations.

An hour later, Lydia entered the U.S. Marshal's Office on the first floor of the Lamar County Courthouse. A female office clerk sat behind a desk in the outer office and looked up as Lydia entered.

"May I help you?" queried the young blonde woman of Lydia.

"Yes, you may. I am Lydia Forsyth and I should like to speak with the Chief United States Marshal. I understand that he is looking to take on a number of Deputies and I have it in mind to be one of them," replied Lydia.

The clerk smiled, but Lydia could tell that the young woman thought it folly for a woman of Lydia's age and attractiveness to become a "rough and tough" Deputy Marshal to trudge the Southern Indian Territory. After all, the Territory was among the most dangerous places in the West and for a woman to ride the wilds in search of elusive criminals was unheard of.

Roseanne Reynolds took a quick breath, brushed a wisp of blonde hair from her forehead, and announced to Lydia, "I'm sorry, but Marshal Franklin is out of the office. He might not be back until late this afternoon."

Lydia smiled at Roseanne, looked around the office and noticed what appeared to be a comfortable chair. She turned to the clerk and politely stated, "That's all right. I'm in no hurry. I'll just sit over here to wait until the Marshal returns." She sat down, opened her handbag, and produced a small book of poetry.

Roseanne held a look of complete surprise on her face. It was quite evident to Roseanne at that moment that Lydia was a person of fortitude, who was determined to succeed in her quest. The shy clerk suddenly felt a pang of admiration for this attractive dark-haired woman. Lydia was unlike any other woman that she knew. She envisioned telling her friends, who would circle around her, the unbelievable news that a woman wanted the job of Deputy Marshal.

Two hours passed before the hallway door of the Marshal's office opened to admit two Deputy U.S. Marshals. They approached Roseanne and the tall, lanky Federal Officer inquired, "Is he in? We have need to speak with him."

Roseanne addressed the Marshal who spoke to her, "I'm sorry, Marshal Bennett. He is out of the office and not expected back for a while yet."

Hearing this news, the two men seemed a bit frustrated to Lydia. They glanced at each other and shrugged before retreating to the door. The Deputy who spoke to the clerk smiled at Lydia as if noticing her for the first time. She smiled back as the two men departed the office.

Time seemed to drag as the railroad wall clock slowly ticked away yet another hour. Lydia closed her eyes for a long moment as she rested her eyes from the text of poetry. The selection that she had open had been among her mother's most favorites, and she it knew by heart. Lydia envisioned,

"How do I love thee, let me count the ways," from Sonnet 43 by Elizabeth Barrett Browning.

Lydia's momentary lull was interrupted by the arrival of William Franklin, the United States Marshal for the Southern District Indian Territory.

She quickly closed her book and slipped it back into her handbag. As Marshal Franklin approached Roseanne at the desk, Lydia stood and called out his name.

"Marshal Franklin! I am Lydia Forsyth and I have been waiting to speak with you, Sir!"

Franklin turned around and quickly appraised the young woman standing before him. "I am a busy man, Miss Forsyth. What business do you have with me?"

The young brunette quickly responded, "Marshal Franklin, I have read that you are seeking to appoint several Deputy U.S. Marshals to serve in the Southern Indian Territory. I should like to speak with you of my qualifications for appointment. I believe I am capable of performing exemplary service for the District Court. I'm unmarried and have no children. I have no qualms about riding into the Territory, and I might add that I am somewhat familiar with the land. My father traveled the Territory as a representative of his company conducting business with several general stores, as well as trading posts within the Choctaw and Chickasaw Nations. On occasion, he allowed me to accompany him."

She watched Franklin's eyes with hopeful heart and should have been disheartened at his curt response.

"Miss Forsyth, although I appreciate your forthrightness, I must tell you that I am, as you stated, looking for Deputies. However, I have sought out only the most formidable men of hearty reputation and possessing unique skills of courage, tracking, horsemanship, and marksmanship. Personally, I doubt that you possess even a novice level of these skills."

The Marshal paused for a long moment to allow Lydia to ponder his words. He continued, "Nonetheless, I stated that I am a busy man. Should you be about later this afternoon, say around four o'clock, I may entertain speaking with you for a few minutes. Now, please excuse me, I have many things to accomplish in my office."

With these last remarks, Franklin entered his office with Roseanne hot on his heels carrying a stack of documents for his signature.

Lydia should have been discouraged, but being the determined, headstrong person that she was, the young woman turned on her heel and exited the Marshal's office. She decided that she needed a lunch and a good cup of coffee and knew exactly where to get one. She walked out of the courthouse and headed toward the Paris town square, intent on returning later that afternoon to speak further with Marshal Franklin.

Lydia reached the center of the Northwest section of the square when a commotion rose from the area of the First National Bank of Paris across the square from her. Women screamed and ran as fast as they could grab their skirts up and dash for the safety of another building. Men ushered their families as best as they could from the immediate vicinity. Horses at hitching racks all around the square reared and bucked against the reins holding them. A few buckboards and other like wagons with people entering the area reined in and taking stock of the situation, attempted to turn their wagons around to escape the escalating pandemonium evolving in the square.

At that instant, five men rushed from the bank, each wearing a bandana covering his face. The men dashed for their horses carrying money sacks loaded with the proceeds of the bank. They fired their revolvers into the air and attempted to mount their waiting horses.

Four of the five men reached their horses and mounted. They turned in the saddle to fire in various directions. Momentarily, gunfire resounded from both armed citizens and arriving lawmen. The last of the five attempted to mount his skittish animal and was hit from several directions by aimed bullets of citizens and Deputies alike as they replied to the outlaw's gunshots.

Lydia observed two of the bank robbers mounted and heading her way. She suddenly realized that they would have to pass close to her to make the river ford and escape into the Indian Territory. Without hesitation, she reached into her handbag and produced her Colt .41 Thunderer and dashed toward the center of the square.

She stood steadfast with revolver in hand, and when the two escaping gunmen were almost upon her, she raised the revolver to line on the first rider and squeezed off her first round.

The outlaw threw up his arms and flailed backward off his mount. The rider-less horse galloped past Lydia as she drew a bead on the second outlaw who by this time leveled his own gun at her. He fired twice as his animal galloped toward the road to safety.

Two bullets whined past Lydia's body to smack into the buildings behind her. She held her Colt as a duelist and squeezed off two rounds herself. The first bullet seared through the outlaw's body and the second round caught him in mid fall from his steed. Again, this horse galloped past her as she stood her ground.

Lydia carefully watched the two fallen outlaws as she approached them. The first man was dead, but the second man still attempted to raise his weapon to fire once again at her. Before he could pull the trigger, she shot him again in the chest and he jerked back with the impact to lie unmoving on the dirt street.

Lydia approached the fallen man and confirmed that she had fired true. Both outlaws were dead. A silence loomed over the Paris town square as the Lamar County Sheriff and his deputies along with U.S. Deputy Marshals surveyed the carnage. None of the five outlaws had made good an escape.

Lydia hovered over the second outlaw that she had killed, reloading her Thunderer, when a voice beside her said, "You were good with that handgun. I watched you. I like your nerve and your ability."

Lydia turned to look into the deep blue eyes of Deputy U.S. Marshal Bennett. An amused smile crossed his face as he further related, "We met briefly in the Marshal's office at the court house, but have not been formally introduced. I am Ross Bennett. I've been a Deputy Marshal for two years now. And, now, just who would you be?"

Lydia blushed a bit as she replied, "I am Lydia Forsyth. I was waiting to speak to Marshal Franklin about becoming a Deputy U.S. Marshal myself. But, he is a busy man and I will probably not be able to convince him of my capabilities for the appointment."

Ross looked over her shoulder a moment, before advising Lydia, "Speak of the devil, here he comes."

U.S. Marshal Bill Franklin momentarily joined them. He looked at

Bennett and then again at Lydia. Bennett nodded his head towards Lydia. Franklin suddenly said, "Bennett, you take over here. Young lady, I want to see you in my office right away. Follow me." He turned and started back towards the Lamar County Courthouse.

Ross grinned at Lydia and said, "He means it! Get going, he's a fast walker."

Lydia slipped the revolver back into her handbag, thankful that the marshals did not confiscate it. She lifted her skirts some and quickly followed Franklin to his office.

As she entered the District U.S. Marshal's Office, she found that Franklin had already entered his office. Roseanne stood behind her desk and pointed to the open doorway. "Go on in," she stated, "he is anxious to speak with you."

Lydia slowly entered William Franklin's office to find him sitting behind his oaken desk. "Have a seat, Miss Forsyth." She took the comfortable chair in front of his desk and looked inquiring at her requester.

Roseanne closed the door to the office and went about her business. Franklin began with, "I also watched as you stood your ground at the square. That was an uncommon display of courage. When other women were fainting and running for cover, you managed to halt the escape of two dangerous men, even as one fired upon you in earnest. That you are a schooled horsewoman is quite evident in that you never flinched as those two wild-eyed animals streaked past you in their panic."

There was a long moment of silence as the Marshal contemplated his next words. "I am inclined to believe your statements in my outer office as we first met. Having witnessed, firsthand, your dedication to law and order, not to mention your marksmanship and steadfast determination, I am empowered to offer you a commission as Deputy United States Marshal of the Southern District Indian Territory. Do you accept?"

Lydia was taken off guard with Franklin's offer. She swallowed hard and then replied, "Marshal Franklin, I would like nothing better than to serve you and this district as a Deputy in your jurisdiction."

Franklin opened a desk drawer and took something in his hand. He rose from his desk and moved to the front of it. He nodded his approval to Lydia and then said, "Raise your right hand and swear in as my deputy."

Lydia rose from her seat, raised her right hand, and repeated the following oath with Marshal Franklin. "I Lydia Forsyth do solemnly swear that I will faithfully execute all lawful precepts to the Marshal of the Southern District Indian Territory under the authority of the United States.......I will support and defend the Constitution of the United States….and I will faithfully discharge the duties of the office I am about to enter: so help me God!"

And, with her final words of oath, United States Marshal William Franklin pinned upon her jacket lapel the Silver Star of Deputy U.S. Marshal. Franklin held out his hand and congratulated his newest Deputy.

He then related his first assignment for her. "It is my direction that you will work with Roseanne for the next two weeks in this office. You are to learn our documentation, distribution, and procedures. I expect that you will do well. After that, either I or my Chief Deputy Marshal will assign you to various duties. For now, please retire for the day and report to this office at eight o'clock tomorrow morning for your first day as my Deputy."

As Lydia turned to exit Marshal Franklin's office, he spoke a second thought, "And, when you wear that Star, I expect you to be armed. It has been said that as soon as someone pins on a Deputy badge, they seem to become a target for every ornery person that totes a gun."

Lydia solemnly nodded her understanding of his words of wisdom. She departed Franklin's office with a smile on her face and faced Roseanne who seemed to be beaming also. Roseanne whispered, "I listened at the doorway. How wonderful for you. I look forward to having you work with me. I shall teach you all that I know."

"Thank you, Roseanne. I also look forward to our working together. I will see you in the morning."

Lydia moved to the outer door of the office and opened it, to suddenly come face to face with a very large black man of rugged looks, and thick mustache. He wore a tie and jacket that covered an obvious handgun at his waist. The Silver Star of Deputy U.S. Marshal was pinned on his shirtfront. He smiled at Lydia with a big toothy grin and said, "Well, Missy! I see that you are sporting a Deputy star also. I am Bass Reeves. Who might you be?"

Lydia had read many stories of this most famous deputy of Judge Issac Parker's court at Fort Smith, Arkansas. She was awestruck in suddenly coming face to face with him, but she replied to his question, "I am Lydia Forsyth. I have read of your exploits in the Indian Territory and your commitment to justice, Marshal Reeves. I have just been sworn in and I want to be the best Lady Marshal that I can. I would love to have conversation with you and glean your advice on traveling the Indian Territory."

Bass Reeves nodded affirmatively with a smile. "As luck would have it, I've been reassigned to the District Court of the Southern Indian Territory at Paris, Texas. I have to testify in court shortly, but I thought I would see Marshal Franklin for a few minutes. Let me know when you have the time, Marshal Forsyth."

"Marshal Forsyth!" That a seasoned Deputy Marshal would address her as such awakened Lydia's mind, and elated as she was, she calmly agreed with Bass and took her leave from the famous lawman. Her dark eyes shined as she walked proudly back to the Peterson Hotel, the Silver Star on her lapel seemingly shined brighter than ever in the afternoon sunlight.

CHAPTER SEVEN

TRAINING THE NEW DEPUTY MARSHAL

Lydia walked directly to her hotel room and closed the door, turned the key to lock it, and then leaned back against it. She exhaled a long sigh of relief and lowered her head as if in prayer. "Thank you, Lord. You have enabled my destiny."

And, with those words, Lydia stepped forward and removed her jacket. She held it proudly in front of her to view the coveted Silver Star of Deputy U.S. Marshal. She closed her eyes and imagined the image that she must cultivate and maintain. In her mind's eye, she was fearless, and dedicated to justice for all people of her jurisdiction. She would conduct herself as such.

Lydia suddenly felt the pangs of hunger. She recalled that due to the circumstances of the commotion on the square, that she did not eat a noon meal. She decided that she would celebrate a bit by partaking of a steak dinner at the café.

She redressed in the same attire as before, and left the badge pinned to her lapel. As a second thought, she again took the Colt .41 Caliber pocket pistol and slipped it into the deep pocket of her skirt. It was intuition that caused her to do so.

Entering the café, Lydia was shown to a small single table by a young brown haired waitress. She proceeded to scan the menu when two obviously drunk male citizens unsteadily entered the establishment. The two men held silly grins on their faces and leered at the patrons within. The tall one reared back and let out a long "Yee Haw! We are hungry and we's looking for fun!"

The young waitress approached the two men. One commented, "Well, George. Look here. We are gonna be served by a pretty gal. You think that she might like a drink with us? I brought our bottle of whiskey." He raised his left hand that held it to prove his intentions.

The other man answered with a slur, "Wes, she just might do that. But, look at the rest of these sour faces. They look like we should not be here. Well, we should show them that we go where we want to go and we always get our way!"

Lynn Phillips, the waitress, attempted to lead the two men to a table way in the back of the café to keep them away from the clientele. However, the two men made commotion every which way as they half stumbled, half walked toward the rear of the café. They shouted insults to staring patrons as they moved.

As they approached Lydia, the two as one suddenly viewed the distinctive star on her lapel. They took in her apparel and decided that she was unarmed and to be taken to task. George Marston grinned at Lydia and then burst into laughter. "Ha, Ha, Ha look at this, Wes. A lady Marshal with a star and she ain't even armed. Now, that is a joke."

Wesley Jones stared at Lydia with blank eyes and bellowed out for all to hear, "Ho, Ho, Lady Marshal! What are you going to do? I suppose you gonna nag us to the jailhouse? You ain't wearing no gun! How you gonna make us behave?"

Lydia calmly laid her menu down on the table and rose from her chair. "I think both of you two gentlemen have had enough fun for tonight. Unless you leave quietly right now, I am arresting you for drunkenness and causing a nuisance."

George laughed at her. "And what makes you think we are going to jail with you?"

At that point Lydia's hand swept from the folds of her skirt and produced her Colt .41 directly into the faces of the two drunken men.

Both men's eyes opened wide and Wes Jones, the second unruly man, blurted out in astonishment, "Holy Mackerel, George! This woman IS armed! And, she's fast with that pistola too!"

Both men raised their hands and due to their drunkenness fell to their knees while still raising their hands high into the air. George slurred out yet another drunken challenge, "Yah, Wes, but she gonna have to drag us to the calaboose. We ain't walking there."

Just at that moment, the door of the café opened and two sheriff's deputies strode into the café. The lawmen stopped a moment and surveyed the sight in front of them. Two drunken citizens were on their knees with hands raised in the aisle of the café with a female holding a revolver on them. The lady wore the Silver Star of Deputy U.S. Marshal on her lapel.

Deputy Sheriff John Lang grinned as he walked up to the situation. "You must be Marshal Forsyth. We got word of your appointment this afternoon over at the jail. We will take over here now, Marshal. You go ahead with your supper. I am glad to meet you."

Lydia sat back down at her table and once again picked up the dinner menu and read over it. The remaining patrons had to take a moment or two before returning to their meals.

Deputies John Lang and Curtis Forbes got the two unruly gentlemen up on their feet and within a few minutes, they were on their way to the Lamar County jail to spend the night and sleep off their overindulgence.

The waitress momentarily appeared at Lydia's table with a fresh cup of hot coffee. She took Lydia's supper order of country fried chicken with mashed potatoes, gravy, and some garden fresh green beans. A couple of biscuits were also in order with some homemade strawberry jam. A supper fit for a queen.

In the background of the café, hushed whispers passed between patrons as they softly discussed the actions of this newly appointed Deputy Marshal. Most of the clientele were duly impressed.

Lydia finished her supper and moved to the front counter to pay for her meal. Lynn Phillips took her supper check and smiled at Lydia. "Marshal, there is no charge for your meal this evening. Thank you for quelling those unruly men. They could have harassed a lot of people in here this evening, but you saved us from their distasteful actions. I'm Lynn Phillips and I'd like you to be my friend. I am usually here serving customers five evenings a week. Perhaps, we could just sit with some coffee sometime and chat a bit. I think that I'd like that."

Lydia smiled back at Lynn, "I am pleased to meet you. I've recently arrived in town and don't really know too many people at this time. We must make time in near future to become further acquainted." The two women shook hands and Lydia decided to walk the square for a bit before retiring for the night.

The night air felt good to Lydia as she strolled around the town square. Her main purpose became to look over the businesses that lined the square and to see how many she could remember from times past. After all, Paris had grown some since the last time she saw it. As she walked, she wondered just how many of her old classmates still resided within the community and what were their livelihoods? Had any of them married and did they have children? She thought that it would be interesting to meet some of them who remembered her and she, them.

Lydia ended her evening walk at the entrance to the Peterson Hotel. She turned and took a parting glance at the town square. Many businesses had changed. A deep breath and long exhale and Lydia went to her room for a night of rest before facing the challenges of her newly acquired position in the morning.

Lydia undressed to her chemise and washed up in the porcelain basin with water poured from the matching pitcher. It was tepid, and felt good to her. She took up a washcloth and used the homemade scented soap bar, raising it her nose for a fragrant moment. Then, she changed into a cotton nightgown and slipped into her bed. She turned to her nightstand and turned out the oil lamp.

She lay back on the soft pillow and reminisced events of the day. Her swearing in as Deputy Marshal brought a smile to her lips. She slipped into a deeper sleep that recalled previous events of her life.

Shadows seemed to move within her mind and Lydia saw an apparition of her friend Annie Schuler dressed as she had been the afternoon they exchanged necklaces. Annie stood silently alone. Unmistakably, Annie was missing the beautiful locket that Lydia had fastened around her neck the last time that she saw her alive.

Lydia's heart beat fast and her breath came in quick inhales and exhales. Then, Annie faded from her view, and there appeared a different vision. This dream depicted a middle-aged woman who was gardening a flower patch in the front of a house. The woman moved this way and that as she carefully weeded the plants.

Lydia saw the rattlesnake coiling up with its head raised to strike. She tried to scream, to warn the woman of the impending danger. Her mouth opened but only silence emerged. Lydia suddenly recognized her mother, Laura Forsyth. The rattler struck its length to the throat of the kneeling Laura and with the garden tool in her hand, the last movement that Laura did was to kill the snake. She fell to earth with her left hand covering the two fang marks at her throat.

Tears streamed down Lydia's face. She woke from this repetitive imagining, pulled bed sheets to her eyes to dry them. She whispered hoarsely, "I love you, Mother." Then that vision faded from her mind. Lydia exhaled a long breath and seemed able to relax slipping further into deep sleep.

Lydia awakened with the dawn and, slipping on her robe, moved silently out of her room and down the dim hallway to the community bathroom. She found that she was the first occupant of the day and partook of a quick bath in the galvanized tub. She found a stack of towels and dried herself off. Re-donning her robe, she quickly returned to her room and prepared herself for her first day of working in the Marshal's office.

She stood in front of the wooden wardrobe and pondered her attire for the day. After selecting a flowing navy skirt, matching jacket, and light blue blouse, she moved to the dresser mirror and began brushing her dark brown hair. She thought about what style she should wear it in, and finally decided upon putting it up above her collar.

After dressing, she stood once more in front of the mirror for a final check. Once satisfied with her appearance, Lydia pinned the Silver Star on her jacket lapel and then reached into the wardrobe to retrieve her gun belt with the Colt .44 Frontier. She strapped it on and settled it comfortably in place around her waist.

Moments later, she exited her room, moved down the hallway and then down the stairs to the hotel lobby. The heels on her high-topped shoes clicked on the wooden floor as she made her way to the hotel entrance and out to the street.

Lydia walked next door to the café and entered. A middle aged, slender brunette in a white apron over a light green dress welcomed her to breakfast and led her to a table half-way into the establishment. She was only a few seats from where she had taken supper the previous evening.

The waitress handed her a breakfast menu and with a smile said, "You must be the new Lady Marshal that I've been hearing about. You are the talk of the town for your actions yesterday. They say that you stopped two bank robbers in the square and arrested a couple of rowdy gents last night. I am most glad that you stopped in here for your morning meal. I am Helen Waters and I'm proud to serve you this morning. Just let me know what you decide on and we'll get right it on out for you."

A few minutes later, Deputy U.S. Marshal Ross Bennett entered the café and glancing around, spotted Lydia at her table. He motioned to Helen that he would join Lydia, "Bring me my usual, Helen. Hope the coffee is good this morning."

Helen replied, "Yes, Ross, the coffee is how you like it – three eggs over easy, skillet potatoes, crispy bacon, and biscuits with honey. Got it! Be right up."

Bennett sauntered up to Lydia and immediately observed the Star on her lapel as well as the belted Colt Revolver around her waist. He commented, "Well, proper Marshal this morning! Yes, Sir, proper Deputy Marshal. May I join you, Marshal Forsyth?"

Lydia looked up from her menu with bright eyes and a smile. "Yes, you may. I'd love some company for breakfast. Do you come here often?"

Ross grinned, "Well, for me, it's the best breakfast in town. Yes, I'm here quite often. The coffee's good and so is the cooking."

Helen stepped to the table asking for Lydia's breakfast order. Lydia looked at Ross and said, "What did you order?"

Helen replied before Ross could answer, "Only the best breakfast on the menu."

Lydia kept her eyes on Ross and answered, "I'll have the same. I feel a bit hungry this morning."

Helen grinned. She felt good that these two Deputy Marshals were becoming acquainted. Ross was a good man and a dedicated Deputy Marshal. They had been friends for a long time, and Helen sensed that he had an aura of loneliness about him. This lady was attractive and once she got to know Ross, Helen felt that they would become fast friends, maybe a bit more. She smiled to herself at that thought.

A few minutes later, Helen served the two Marshals and left them to their breakfasts and conversation while she continued to serve and welcome other patrons.

Lydia started the conversation, "Marshal Bennett, where do you hail from? I am Lydia Forsyth. I was born here in Paris and lived here until I was about sixteen. My father represented his company's wares throughout the county, and throughout the Choctaw Nation to various trading posts and general stores. After my mother passed on, he sent me to Dallas where I attended the Ladies Academy until I graduated and now, here I am."

Bennett replied, "I'm Ross Bennett. Please call me Ross. I grew up in Fort Smith, Arkansas. My Pa was a Deputy Marshal for Judge Parker. One day he rode into The Territory and never came back. He was never found, although many have searched for him. Ma and I figured a long time ago that he perished on his mission. We think he died either from an accident or he is one of those murdered with his remains hidden from sight. Anyway, I grew up hunting and fishing. I learned to track animals and most anything. A friend of my father, another Marshal, took me under his wing, so to speak, and educated me in the use of handguns."

Lydia swallowed hard as she found the words to reply, "My father took his final ride into the Territory and was caught in a tremendous thunder storm. He made it back to Paris, but came down with pneumonia. He never recovered. I buried him in Paris two years ago. After that, I continually boarded at the school until completion, and then I read about the need for Marshals here in Paris with the newly formed circuit court. I came back here to wear the Star and to ride the Territory as a Deputy Marshal. I want justice for folks in need."

After breakfast, the two federal officers walked together to the courthouse. Several citizens on the street took curious note of the young female with the belted revolver.

Ross and Lydia arrived at the courthouse and Lydia continued on to the District U.S. Marshal's office. Ross had business with the Lamar County Court and proceeded to the next floor.

Lydia entered the Marshal's office to find Roseanne already there and at work. They exchanged greetings, and then Roseanne introduced Lydia to the desk that she would occupy during her tenure with the office.

Pointing to a pile of papers, Roseanne began, "Lydia, these documents are the most important ones for Marshal Franklin to view each day. These are the warrants issued from the District Federal Court upstairs. He reviews each of these warrants and then assigns the Deputy he feels best to serve the warrant."

She continued, "He likes the warrants to be organized by severity of the case. In other words, the most severe charges such as murder and robbery are at the top of the stack with lesser charges, such as illegal whiskey to the bottom of the stack."

Lydia acknowledged with a nod of her head. Roseanne then gave Lydia the stack of warrants and directed, "Read through the warrants and familiarize yourself with the format. Over time, you will recognize the same names over several warrants. That's because the person named is still at large and is still doing illegal activities."

Roseanne bid Lydia to sit at the desk and familiarize herself with the format of the documents. Following that, she introduced her trainee to the morning receipt of new wanted posters. She explained where the posters originated, and what disposition was made of them.

It was an informative two-week internship that Lydia served with Roseanne. Best of all, they became friends. Lydia explained her background and Roseanne related hers, "I was raised on a farm in the country. I worked hard to learn reading, writing, and arithmetic. I read all the books I could find about history, geography, and administration. Most of the girls in my community married boys from the same area at around sixteen or seventeen. Within a year, they had babies. I didn't want that yet. I wanted to find my way in the world without having to work a farmer's wife's life. I wanted to work in a city. So, I learned office work and found that I love doing it. Now, I work here and I have friends that work in other offices around town."

For Lydia, the office opportunity also afforded her the opportunity to meet most of the Deputies under Marshal Franklin. These men were her peers with whom she'd be working as she evolved toward serving warrants, writs, and making arrests.

She also had opportunity to inquire of Bass Reeves as to how he was so successful apprehending criminals in the Territory. Reeves explained his method, "Well now, them that is wanted knows that I'm a-coming for them. So, I disguises myself to get as close to them as possible before they recognize me. It works well with the surprise."

She also asked his advice as to how she should travel the Nations. He took a long look at her and after pondering his response, stated, "You should also disguise. I say to you—dress like and act like a man. You must have a good rifle. I suggest a Winchester Rifle. Get yourself a good spirited hoss and always trust in his instincts. Learn the country and travel with eyes in the back of your head. Be alert to everything around you, especially nature sounds. You do that, you might just live to see another day."

Lydia related her appreciation to the famous lawman before he departed with his current warrants from the court in his grip.

"Thank you so much Marshal Reeves. I shall keep your advice close to hand and heart."

Reeves bowed slightly before departing her presence. He stepped out into the outer courthouse hallway and left Paris, Texas.

CHAPTER EIGHT

A HORSE FOR LYDIA

Lydia completed her first two weeks as Deputy Marshal working in the District Marshal's office. Roseanne often complimented her on how quickly she learned all about writs, warrants, and distribution of the various official documents. She also spent time sitting in federal court as a spectator during a trial. Specific to her interest was observing Deputies as sworn witness for the prosecution.

Now, the time had arrived for her to pair up with a seasoned Marshal in order to carry out her duties. U.S. Marshal Franklin called Lydia into his office to announce her next phase of training. He asked, "Do you have a suitable mount yet?

Lydia advised, "No, Marshal Franklin. I don't have a horse at this time."

Franklin grinned, "I expect that all of my Deputies should have a trustworthy mount on which to conduct business. Take this day and search out an animal of your choosing. Insure that it is steady, well trained, and spirited. We need these qualities in our closest friend in the wilderness."

Lydia took her leave of the Marshal and inquired of the office clerk, Roseanne, "Where would I find an appropriate mount and trappings?"

Roseanne was a world of knowledge. "I would begin at Martin's Livery & Stables. Besides the usual livery rental horse, he often has recently broken animals brought in from various ranches and horse hunters in the area. If he doesn't have what you are looking for, he would know just where to inquire next."

Lydia grinned as she replied, "Thanks for that information, Roseanne. You always amaze me with your knowledge." Roseanne smiled in return.

Lydia exited the courthouse and sought out Frank Sutton, the taxi driver. She found him parked in front of the Peterson Hotel. She approached and greeted her former classmate with a pleasant "Good morning, Frank. Would you please take me to Martin's Livery?"

Frank helped her up to sit beside him in the driver's seat and clucked to his team. "What you going to Martin's for?"

"Well, it seems that I have need of a horse. I've been advised that he is the man to check with."

Frank nodded his agreement, and then offered his own thoughts, "If Martin doesn't have a suitable animal, let me know. I have friends that are in the wild horse business and they've recently brought a dozen or so animals back with them."

Lydia reflected on Frank's suggestion. It echoed what Roseanne had said.

The taxi arrived at Martin's Livery and Stables. Frank drew his team to the hitching post near the entrance and tied up. He turned to Lydia, "I'll step inside with you. I know Joseph and he will be anxious to assist you."

The duo entered Martin's office together, Frank slightly ahead of her. Joseph Martin looked up from behind his small wooden desk and grinned as he recognized Frank Sutton. He rose and stepped out into the office area to hold out his hand in greeting to his friend. "Frank! This is a surprise. I thought you had enough animals to run your taxi business. What can I help you with today?"

Frank exchanged handshakes with Joseph saying, "I don't need anything today, Joe. My long time friend here, Marshal Forsyth, is in need of a gallant steed for her profession."

Joseph seemed to focus on Lydia for the first time since she and Frank entered his office. Joe, momentarily awestruck by the Silver Star on her lapel and by the fact that she was armed, quickly recovered his composure and smiled warmly at Lydia as he held out his hand to welcome her to his establishment. He had heard about her. She took his hand and returned his welcome greeting.

"Marshal Forsyth. You must be the new lady lawman that holds the town's immediate interest and curiosity. Everyone is talking about your shoot out in the town square a few weeks ago. I am glad to make your acquaintance. Frank says that you need a horse. What do you have in mind?"

"I need a trustworthy animal. One that is spirited, yet well trained. I would say about fourteen to fifteen hands, and solid for long rides over rough terrain."

Joe Martin took only an instant to reply. "I believe that I might just have the horse you seek. Come on back to my corrals. I have recently acquired a bay gelding, about three years old that might just fit your bill. He's of very high spirits, and somewhat unpredictable. It would take a highly experienced rider to handle him."

"I am that," Lydia replied.

Frank and Lydia followed Joe Martin through his office and out into his holding area where several animals moved aimlessly around the enclosed corral. Still, Joe led them to another corral out a bit further.

Finally, Joe Martin stopped and climbed the bars of a corral. "I keep this one here because of his nature. Most folks come to me seeking a gentle horse. This young one is quite the handful. No one seems able to handle him yet."

Lydia climbed the corral bars to peer out at a single bay animal. He was magnificently statured. The animal stood leisurely munching at a feedbox filled with hay. He turned slowly to peer at the humans that had suddenly invaded his personal space and he slowly walked on up to them. He snorted at Joseph and Frank, but turned his interest to a new scent, Lydia. He stood for long moments, seemingly to take in her womanly aura.

Lydia did not flinch. She stood her ground with the bay right at her body. She slowly reached out and lightly stroked the bay's face. He lowered his head. He seemed to like her touch. Lydia inquired, "May I enter this corral?"

Joe exhaled long before answering her, "Yes, you may, but I will tell you again. This animal is unpredictable."

Lydia paid him no attention. She stepped down from the corral bars and entered the arena through the gate, closing it behind her. The bay watched her with curiosity. Lydia walked to the center of the corral and turned to face the horse.

She stood motionless watching the bay carefully. The animal seemed restless. The bay lifted his head to sniff the air, and then reared up, shaking his head with hooves pawing the air to show he had no fear of any human. Lydia stood her ground, not moving from her spot.

They stood face to face, each eyeing the other. It seemed like an eternity to Lydia. Still, she remained unmoving.

Slowly, the bay approached her and lowered his head. She reached out to touch his nose, and then gently rubbed his face and neck.

After several long minutes, the dark-haired Lady turned and walked to the corral gate where Frank and Joseph stood with total amazement on their faces as the bay followed Lydia up to the gate.

Lydia looked at Joe Martin, "I will need saddle and other trappings. What do you want for this horse?"

Martin was awestruck, but replied, "I still don't believe it. I've never seen that horse react to anyone like he just did with you. I'll sell it to you for the same as I bought it. I paid fifty dollars for the animal because his owner was desperate to get shuck of him. He couldn't handle him."

Martin paused for a moment before continuing, "Saddle, blanket, bridle, and other tack, I'd ask another twenty five dollars."

Lydia grinned at Martin. "Write up the bill of sale, Mr. Martin. And, I would also board my newly acquired mount at your livery. We can discuss the terms of that option when you present me with the ownership papers tomorrow morning." Lydia held her hand out, and Joseph Martin shook hands with her to seal the deal. Lydia now had her own mount. She would take her first ride with him the next day.

Lydia turned to Frank. "Well, Frank, let's go back to the courthouse. I've got news to pass on."

Early the next morning, Lydia rose early. Today, she had a chore to do and she knew it. Today, she would ride her newly acquired mount. She had made a good choice, but now she had to prove that her decision was worthwhile.

After washing up with the soap, basin, and water from the pitcher in her room, Lydia went to the wardrobe and looked over her clothes. She would dress differently this day. She selected a plain brown split riding skirt with dark blue men's shirt. She pulled on her riding boots and then opened her travel trunk again. She withdrew a worn dark grey cowboy hat, and a dark blue and white polka dot silk bandana. She tied the bandana loosely around her neck and donned the hat.

Finally, Lydia stood in front of the mirror to appraise her attire for the task at hand. She knew that she was in for a grand ride this morning and she was dressed for the event.

This was not a task for the wearing of the Star nor would she wear her Colt Revolver. This was not an official duty, but one of a more personal nature.

After locking her room, Lydia went down the stairs and across the lobby to the street outside. Frank was there as he had promised and after climbing up to the seat beside him, Lydia motioned forward saying, "Let's go to Martin's. I have a meeting with a new friend."

Frank looked Lydia up and down, silently studying her attire, and just shook his head. This old friend of his was full of surprises. She now resembled a woman horse wrangler, rather than a Deputy Marshal.

The horse taxi drew up in front of Martin's Livery and Stables. Frank tied his team to the hitching post and turned to Lydia. "I wouldn't miss this for the world." Lydia gave him a demure smile and replied, "Well, Frank, there are a lot of things that you don't know about me. Maybe you will find out one of them this morning. Come, I've a ride to make."

They entered Martin's office and he was surprised at Lydia's attire. He remarked, "Miss Forsyth, I've not had the bay saddled and ready for you yet."

Lydia grinned and replied, "I know I'm early. I didn't expect you to have him saddled and ready to go. That's my job. I presume that you have the saddle and other necessities ready at hand. Let's go back to meet my new friend."

Joe Martin led the way to the rear corral where the bay stood quietly munching hay. When the humans assembled at his corral, the animal instantly knew something was up. He turned to face the intruders.

Joe showed Lydia the saddle and trappings. She inspected all of it before remarking, "This is fair enough." She lifted the saddle and blanket on one hand and the bridle in the other and strode to the gate to the corral. She opened it and stepped inside.

Lydia dropped the saddle beside the entrance and closed the gate. Then, she walked to the center of the arena and stood as she had done the previous day. The bay turned to face her. This was a new figure for him so he lifted his head and reared to paw the air. His nostrils flared as he caught the scent of the woman before him.

Unbeknownst to Lydia, U.S. Marshal Franklin had just arrived at the livery. He sought out Joe Martin. As he approached Martin and Sutton, the duo turned to meet him. Both put fingers to their lips, a signal to remain silent and watch the woman with the horse in the corral.

Franklin peered over the corral bars and nodded his understanding. The three men watched intently as the Lady Marshal worked her magic on the unpredictable animal.

At the center of the corral, the bay shook his head up and down and moved toward the woman standing before him. Once again, he lowered his head and she stroked his face and spoke softly to him. "They tell me that you are unpredictable. You don't even know what that means. I need you to be trustworthy for me. Today, you and I will find the spirit of each other and merge our strong spirits as one. We will be a team, you and I."

Lydia ran her hands over the bay's whole body, gently. She ran her hand down each leg to pick up his hooves one by one, cleaning each with a pick from her pocket. After that, she faced him with bridle in hand. The horse stepped to her and took the bit as though they had done this hundreds of times before.

Lydia slowly slipped the bit into the bay's mouth and the bridle into place over his head. She continued to stroke the animal's neck and speak softly to him. She turned and, taking the reins leaving a lot of play, began walking toward the corral gate. The bay followed in her footsteps.

At the corral entrance, Lydia looped the reins loosely over one bar of the corral. The bay did not flinch. She let out a short sigh of relief.

Next, she reached down and lifted the saddle blanket and placed it on the animal's back, adjusting it to best position. The gelding had been saddled before, standing in place for her.

Then, she picked up the saddle and with a quick movement placed it on the bay's back. The bay turned his head to look at her and she quietly spoke to him, "Easy now. I know that you have had this on your back before. You know what this is."

The bay stood calm and motionless while she adjusted the saddle, tightened the cinches, and adjusted the stirrups to her satisfaction. When she was ready, Lydia led the bay to the center of the corral. Once there, she stopped and stroked the bay's face, neck, and spoke softly to it. Then, she took a deep breath and with reins in hand, she put foot to stirrup and rose into the saddle.

No sooner had Lydia settled into the saddle than the bay decided to show his contrary side. He rose up on hind legs to come down on all fours and move into a challenging bucking contest.

The three men watching from the corral bars quickly inhaled with surprise, as Lydia was tossed hither and yon. She stayed with the unruly gelding, raking his flanks with her boot heels and yelling encouragement to keep bucking. "Aw, come on now! You can do better than that! Show me some real wild! Give me your best!"

It seemed to the three observers that they once or twice heard a wild "Yahoo!" emanate from the exuberant lady riding the wild cyclone in the center of the arena.

A few moments later, a wicked twister movement by the bay sent Lydia sprawling to the ground. The three men started for the corral gate but stopped when she rose from the dust and ran the still bucking animal down, to grab loose reins and the saddle horn and swing back up into the saddle again.

Twenty minutes later, the bay seemed to run out of steam and slowed to a walk around the corral, the lady buckaroo guiding him and putting him through various calculated moves. The bay completely obeyed her wishes, and as they approached the gate, Lydia slid out of the saddle and dropped the reins.

The horse trailed after her to finally place his face to her shoulder and receive her soothing words. "Well, now, that was some burst of emotion. You've got the spirit, but we'll have to work on your manners. That was no way to treat a lady."

Lydia gaily laughed while she stroked the bay's face and neck. A thought hit her at that time, and she took the bay's face in her hands and looked directly into his eyes. I think it is time that you got a name. You are now my best friend, Chester. Yes, I think Chester fits you well."

Marshal Franklin turned to Joe and Frank with, "Well now, my new law Lady Marshal is certainly full of surprises."

Lydia stripped the saddle and other gear off the bay and turned Chester loose to roam his personal corral. She opened the gate and stepped through it, closing it behind her.

She came face to face with Marshal Franklin who greeted her with, "Marshal Forsyth, that was some display of horsemanship. I am confident that you are an accomplished horsewoman. I think that you are ready. Be at the courthouse with your mount at about ten o'clock tomorrow morning to assist Deputy Marshal Bennett in serving several federal warrants around the Paris area. You are assigned to field duty as of now."

Franklin then smiled at her for the first time while giving her an approving nod of his head. With a short wave, he turned and left the livery for business elsewhere.

Lydia could hardly contain herself. She was now assigned to field duty as Deputy U.S. Marshal. Her face beamed with excitement. Her dark eyes glowed with delight, and best of all, she thought, "Yes! I am accepted for my abilities and demeanor. I shall be the best Deputy Marshal that I can."

CHAPTER NINE

SERVING WRITS AND WARRANTS

Lydia was dressed in her brown riding skirt and sky blue blouse with leather vest and calf-high riding boots with silver spurs as she leisurely rode Chester from Martin's Livery to the courthouse on this warm morning. The sun shined bright on the Silver Star pinned on her vest. Around her waist was her cartridge belt with holster and her short-barreled Colt .44. She was ready to perform the day's tasks of assisting Deputy Marshal Bennett serve warrants and arrest those criminals whose names were on them.

Chester, the once unmanageable horse, seemed eager to please his new mistress who treated him with affection, yet respect. He obeyed her every whim and direction.

Arriving at the courthouse, Lydia took note of the saddled sturdy appaloosa at the hitching post. She correctly surmised that it was Marshal Bennett's mount. She guided Chester up beside the animal and dismounted. She looped the reins around the hitching rail leaving enough play for Chester to partake of a drink from the water trough if desired. The appaloosa raised his head for a moment to appraise the newcomers and then went back to quenching his thirst.

Lydia entered the courthouse, spurs lightly jingling to her steps. She walked directly to the District Marshal's Office and entered. Roseanne waved a welcoming to her and smiled. She motioned to the Marshal's office door and bid her to enter.

"They are expecting you, even as you are a bit early."

Lydia stepped to the door, knocked once, and entered to join Marshal Franklin and Deputy Marshal Bennett reviewing a small sheath of legal documents. Bennett called out a name with charge and Franklin checked it off on his matching list.

One name caught Lydia's attention right away. Bennett stated, "Gabe Johnson – Murder Suspect" and Franklin replied with an audible "Check."

Lydia's mind immediately went back ten years to the murder of her friend Annie and her family. "Could he be the one that got away back then?" She swallowed hard at the thoughts that raged through her mind.

It took a few moments for her to regain her composure and listen to the remainder of the warrants that ranged from possession of stolen federal property to federal bank robbery suspect." She surely had not thought of the various ranges of federal violations that the Paris Circuit Court would issue arrest warrants for.

The list complete, Deputy Marshal Bennett turned to Lydia and grinned. "Well, do you think you are ready for a bit of real law work?"

Lydia nodded her head and replied, "This is just what I've been waiting to experience. I'm ready to start earning my pay."

Bennett looked into her eyes and, nodding, said, "All right then, Marshal Forsyth, let's go out there and see what we can do to serve all ten of these federal summons and warrants today."

The two deputies walked side by side out the door of the Marshal's office and to the hitching rack in front of the courthouse where they mounted their animals. "Where to first?" inquired Lydia.

"I thought we'd ride out to the Charles Duncan farm first. It's within a few miles and it's only a writ for summons. Duncan presumably observed someone attempting to sell a few U.S. Army horses. He stated that he saw the U.S. brand on the shoulders of both, and can identify the man who had the animals."

Lydia seemed to recall the name Duncan from the distant past. She wondered if Duncan was the same person that attended school with her.

The two Deputy Marshals rode out of Paris, Texas in a southwesterly direction. Lydia watched the landscape as they rode. There were several fields of cotton and she recalled that Paris was a major cotton exchange site. Farmers would bring their crops of cotton into Paris and sell it to the cotton exchange for the current sales rate.

About forty-five minutes into the ride, Bennett motioned to Lydia to draw up and side with him. They let their mounts take a few minutes breather while he pointed out the Duncan farm in the near distance.

"We'll ride in together slowly. I image that Duncan will meet us before we get to his doorstep. Let me do the talking. Just watch and see how we handle this sort of writ serving."

Lydia acknowledged her understanding with a nod of her head and a short "I will."

After a few minutes, the law duo resumed their ride into the entrance of Duncan's land. The farm appeared prosperous and well cared for. Nearing the main house, a tall man in bibbed overalls and dark gray shirt left the door and stepped out to the hitching post and water trough to greet this pair of visitors.

Charles Duncan shaded his eyes against the noonday sun as he watched the couple ride towards him. He immediately recognized Deputy U.S. Marshal Bennett but could not recall the young woman riding with him. Once the couple got within fifty feet of him, he made out the glint of a Silver Star on the woman also. He was somewhat taken back with this sight. He had never seen a female Deputy Marshal before.

"Hallo, Duncan!" called out Deputy Marshal Bennett.

"Hallo, yourselves!" called back Charles, "Who is the lady traveling with you?"

A long moment passed as the riders closed the distance to stop in front of Charles Duncan. "My partner here is Deputy Marshal Forsyth. She's assisting me this day in serving federal court documents."

The name "Forsyth" surged through Duncan's mind and his eyes suddenly gleamed with understanding. He looked up at Lydia and remarked, "Marshal Forsyth! Forsyth! Is that you, Lydia? It's been a month of Sundays since I've seen you. I thought you moved to Fort Worth or such about maybe four years ago."

Lydia smiled and replied, "Yes, Charles. It's me, Lydia. I see that you've taken care of your father's farm. How is he these days?"

Duncan answered, "He ain't none the worse for wear, but too worn out to farm anymore. I've a room in the back of the house for him. And, you might also remember my wife. I married Jenny Donahue. She's already borne me one son and a daughter. The children are staying at a neighbor farm. They should be back sometime tomorrow."

Duncan continued in a prideful manner, "We are expecting our next child any day now and Jenny tells me that it must be another son."

Lydia responded, "I remember Jenny. I think she must make you a wonderful wife. She always said that she wanted to stay here around Paris and marry a farming man."

At that very instant, Jenny appeared in the doorway holding her stomach and yelling to Duncan. "It's time, Charles! This baby is coming now!"

Duncan immediately looked frantic. "Oh Lord! I haven't got the midwife here yet! I don't know what to do. Always before, there was a mid-wife here to help Jenny."

Lydia turned to Bennett, "We've got this to do!" and without another word, she dismounted and rushed to Jenny who looked up into her eyes and remarked, "Lydia? Is that you?"

Lydia smiled warmly at Jenny and took her arm to guide her back into her bedroom. "Yes, Jenny. It is me. I am going to help you with your birthing. Let's do this together. We can do this."

Jenny nodded and allowed Lydia to assist her into the interior of the house telling her how to get to her bedroom for birthing."

Marshal Bennett dismounted quickly also and tied his mount and Chester to the hitching post at the water trough. He looked deeply into Duncan's eyes and saw the concern. He grinned somewhat as he spoke, "Ladies been having babies for a long time. Don't you worry, there's two friends in there having a life experience. Well, we got to wait it out. I think we should sit out here on your porch and have a smoke."

Duncan thought hard for a long minute or so. "I'd like a smoke. In fact, I've got about half a jug of homemade beer if you'd like a taste. Would you join me in a cup of beer?"

Bennett nodded and reached to his vest pocket to produce a pack of store bought cigarettes and a small box of sulfur matches.

Duncan reappeared with a jug and two tin cups. He poured a measure of homemade beer into each and handed one to Bennett who reciprocated by lighting two cigarettes and handing one to Duncan.

For the next hour, the two men smoked cigarettes and softly spoke about farming and especially about raising cotton. Bennett, of course, listened while he let Duncan ramble on about his farming experience.

Lydia got Jenny onto her bed and after lifting Jenny's skirts found that she was quite ready to deliver. She held Jenny's hand and asked, "You got something to quell the pains? You've been through this twice already, talk to me about it."

Jenny pointed out a length of hard leather that laid on the nightstand next to the bed and Lydia reached up and handed to her. Jenny took it into her mouth and bit down hard as the next birthing pain reached her.

At that point, Lydia began singing softly one of the only hymns that she knew, "Come thy fount of every blessing…."

Jenny began breathing in unison with Lydia's soft rendition of the song. After several long minutes, she let out a shriek and grabbed the bedposts tightly as the baby began its birth.

Lydia kept singing and her words became louder and more hoarse as Jenny moaned and screamed while the baby moved slowly from her birthing channel.

Several minutes later, Lydia eased the newborn from it from the mother as Jenny took a final hard push and lay exhausted from the delivery. Lydia smiled as she peered down at the child and turning it over, took a quick smack up the child's back to produce an initial inhale and sudden outburst of crying. She looked over at Jenny and announced, "What do you name your new son?"

Quickly, Lydia tied the umbilical cord in two places with thread sitting ready on the table by the bed. Between the two ligatures, she cut the cord.

Jenny looked up at her with very tired eyes and a slight smile. "I think we had decided on Joshua. Yes, that's it. Joshua Duncan."

Lydia used the cooled water from the stove and clean rags to wash young Joshua. Then, she wrapped the baby in the waiting blanket. Lydia handed the newborn to Jenny who looked down on him with love in her eyes and then took him to her breast and held him dearly to her heart.

Lydia spoke softly to Jenny, "My job is finished here. I will bring

Charles in to you. Who is your mid-wife? Where can I find her and tell her to come quickly to finish the procedure of birth?"

Jenny replied, "Rachel Jordan. She lives on the next farm down the road to the left. Thank you, Lydia. I remember you from school. I am glad that you were here with me as I had this baby."

Lydia smiled down at her and giving Jenny a soft wave of her hand, left the room and went to the front porch to announce the news to the nervous waiting gentlemen. She stepped out on to the porch with a grin and a good feeling within her to announce, "Charles Duncan, you have another son. His name is Joshua Duncan and his mother wishes your presence immediately."

Duncan was so overwhelmed that he jumped up and dropped his mug of beer. He almost fell off the porch, and had it not been for Bennett catching him and setting him straight, he would have.

After making it to the door, the new father entered his home.

Lydia turned to Bennett and mentioned, "I think that I should put some coffee on the stove. I could use a cup myself. After Charles comes back from seeing his newest child we should serve him the summons and ride down the road to notify the mid-wife to quickly come to their aid."

Bennett agreed, "I could use some coffee myself." He grinned at Lydia saying, "I learn more about you every day. You done good here today."

Lydia sort of blushed a bit and replied with a quiet "Thank you."

Duncan returned about half an hour later to have a coffee with his federal visitors. Lydia handed Charles the summons, "Charles Duncan, you are hereby served with notice to appear as a witness before the district court in Paris, Texas at one o'clock on the twentieth of this month, that being two weeks hence. Do you understand this Writ of Summons?"

Duncan nodded his understanding and stated his acceptance of the writ.

As an afterthought, Lydia asked Duncan the next question on her mind. "Charles, do you know or have you even heard of a man called Gabe Johnson?

Lydia's question caught Charles off guard. He owed the Marshals for their help, but he didn't want to get involved with whatever misdeeds Gabe Johnson had committed.

Charles thought for a long moment and then looked at Lydia to remark, "I've heard the name, but I don't know this person."

After another moment, he more honestly stated "Come to think about it, I seem to remember someone tell me that while out hunting some wild turkey, he thought that he saw this Gabe Johnson feller riding hell bent towards the old Elliott cabin, about four miles upstream along the river. That's all I remember."

Bennett and Lydia thanked Charles for the information and before mounting up, advised that they would notify Rachel Jordan to come to their farm as quickly as possible. The law duo waved farewell to Duncan and continued on their way.

As soon as they were out of earshot, Bennett turned to Lydia to ask, "What made you ask Charles about this Gabe person?"

She replied, "It was just a quick hunch that crossed my mind. Why do you ask?"

"I think we will just leave the rest of our writs for tomorrow and pursue this latest news that Gabe Johnson may be lurking around within ten miles of Paris. It shouldn't take us long to reach that cabin and investigate it."

Lydia agreed, and together, after informing Rachel of the new arrival, spurred their animals into a quick cantor towards the Red River.

CHAPTER TEN

A MURDERER ESCAPES

Towards late afternoon, the air was still warm as Deputy Marshals Forsyth and Bennett neared the old dwelling along the banks of the Red River called Elliott's Cabin. They slowed their mounts to a walk, taking care to pay close attention to their surroundings.

The landscape was covered with thick brush, tall grasses, and dense stands of trees. They finally reached a point where Bennett motioned for them to dismount and go forward on foot.

After securing their animals to some slender trees, they stealthily approached to within fifty yards of the run down building. Not a soul was in sight. The lean-to on the right side of the dilapidated building appeared empty.

The pair of deputies listened carefully for the tell tale signs of nature. The air was humid and still. Something seemed amiss. There were no birds calling to each other in song. Nor were there any tiny creatures deemed scurrying away from their presence. The other obvious missing sound was that of frogs croaking along the brush-obscured riverbank, some twenty yards toward the rear of the cabin. In fact, it appeared that the only movement was the periodic swarm of insects that seemed to enjoy making a nuisance of themselves.

Bennett took a deep breath, and drawing his revolver, motioned Lydia to work her way to the right side of the yard. He would go to the left and the two of them would move toward the closed door of the shanty.

Lydia nodded, drew her revolver, and moved silently about fifteen yards to the right. They looked at each other, nodded, and moved slowly forward to converge on the cabin door.

Lydia was somewhat aligned with the lean-to when the still air issued forth a quick mechanical sound. In the next instant, a rifle spit hot lead toward the lady law officer. The bullet whined past her right ear and in the next moment, Lydia fired her own reply to the perpetrator.

Bennett dashed quickly to the corner of the shack and, peering around it, saw the quick flash of someone running toward the river. A second later, the brush between the cabin and the river crackled and flared up suddenly in hot flames and smoke.

One sound echoed above the crackling of the brush fire. It was the wild yell of someone shouting "Come on, you crow bait! Go!" and then, a loud splash as a horse and rider evidently jumped into the water to swim the river to the Indian Territory side. The elusive suspect was gone and there was nothing that either of the two deputies could do at this point except inspect the shanty.

Carefully opening the cabin door, homemade hinges slightly squeaked and then Bennett had the door wide open. The duo entered and on the floor was the body of a middle-aged red-haired man. He lay on his back, arms out flung, unseeing eyes wide with surprise. A bullet hole was centered over his heart and he lay in a pool of his own blood.

Bennett carefully examined the man. At last, he looked up at Lydia and remarked, "I've seen this man in Paris recently. Perhaps, maybe, last week. I'll bet that he's the bounty hunter seeking to bring in our suspected murderer named Gabe Johnson. Well, it looks a lot like Johnson just escaped us. This man will not hunt criminals again."

Lydia nodded. She thought, "I wish that I'd just been able to see his face before he lit out. Well, maybe we will go into the Territory and seek him out."

Bennett asked Lydia, "Look over there in the corner. Is that some blankets or a bed roll?" She stepped over to the corner and indeed it was a bedroll. She replied to that effect.

He then said, "Well, we've got to roll this fella up in it and take him back to town to the undertaker. He'll take care of him. There doesn't seem to be any other animals around except for ours, so I'll rig a travois and we'll drag him back to the nearest farm. Once there, we'll see about securing a horse, mule, or wagon to transport him the rest of the way to Paris.

Lydia had the job of rolling the deceased up in the bedroll. She spread the roll out on the floor and Bennett helped her drag the body onto the blankets. Then, he went outside and with his sheath knife, cut some sturdy thin young trees and, hacking off the branches, fashioned two poles for the travois. He found some other sturdy fallen limbs and likewise stripped the smaller branches off them. He cut long grasses and twisted them into a sort of hemp type ropes, which he used to tie cross bars onto the long poles.

He noticed that the brush fire had consumed itself and had burned itself out. The area from the rear of the shack to the river was now plainly in view, although blackened by the fire.

After an hour's work, the travois was ready. Bennett turned to Lydia, "Go and bring our horses up here to the cabin. I'll drag our passenger to his transportation mode."

Lydia found both mounts exactly where they had left them, and both animals were glad to see her. She untied them and led them first to the makeshift water trough in front of the cabin allowing both horses to drink of whatever water remained.

Bennett turned to Lydia and inquired, "Do you want to drag the travois, or be the look out?"

"Well, Bennett. Chester needs to learn some things as we go along. I'll take the travois with us. Show me and talk me through this. Chester and I can do this."

Bennett acknowledged her wishes and, with Lydia's assistance, placed the poles of the travois through Chester's stirrups and tied them there with lengths of rope from her lariat. Chester felt the strange weight on the saddle but she was not mounted yet. He wondered about that, looking cautiously around at Lydia preparing to mount. Once mounted, Chester felt the extra weight but felt comfortable that his lady was with him.

The small parade turned toward the Sherman Road and their initial goal, the first farm that they came upon. Dusk fell and the deputy duo had to stop for the night. They unlimbered Chester's burden and hobbled both mounts to let them forage through the tall grasses along the road.

They lit a small fire, and Bennett offered up thick pieces of beef jerky to dine on. The only liquid was water in their canteens. When the moon reached a peak in the sky, the duo rolled up in their blankets and slept somewhat until the light of morning.

Orrin Waters was the eldest of five boys and two girls that grew up in West Virginia. From a young age, he wanted to have his own land and marry a farm savvy young woman. At the age of nineteen, he left his family and home behind him and traveled to Paris, Texas where he engaged in various odd jobs. He saved his hard-earned cash in a local bank.

After a year or so, he met a young red-haired woman named Cassie Hodges. They seemed interested in each other from the start. Orrin escorted Cassie to community affairs and they attended church together in Paris.

After a reasonable time, he asked her to be his wife. She took him to her parents who were cotton farmers, and he requested permission marry their daughter. They were overjoyed that a thrifty young man of Orrin's caliber would ask their daughter's hand. Soon after, they married.

Orrin and Cassie lived with her parents for six months, when one day observing the Saturday Market Day in the Paris Town Square, he made a strange observation. It seemed that most of the farmers' wagons bore cotton, the financial mainstay of the area.

Orrin's attention was drawn more toward the minor sales that the farmers' wives peddled from their own small wagons during these days.

He noticed that the farmers' wives were selling eggs, butter, and chickens for butcher. Although Orrin had seen the wives with their wares before, it was as if he was seeing them in a different light. That gave him an idea that would transform his life and provide a living for him and his bride. The enterprising young man decided to pursue that idea.

Within a week or so, he had secured a small piece of land along the Red River, where the land was fertile enough and they could build a small house and pursue his dream.

The only drawback was that the land lay four miles from Paris and it would take a few hours to travel to the market place on the square.

That was fine with him. He discussed his idea with Cassie and they agreed. That was what they wanted to do.

Over the next few years, Orrin and Cassie built a small farm that grew vegetables for their table, and they raised various roasting and frying chickens. Orrin got excited one day as he captured a few live wild turkeys in some homemade traps and decided to attempt to raise them for eating purposes also.

Their small farm become known for plump turkey, and chickens, which the population of Paris looked forward to purchasing on market days. Cassie always had several dozen prize eggs to sell on the side.

They took whatever vegetables, carrots, snap beans, and such, as they could spare from their own pantry. They made a comfortable enough living through their efforts.

On this crisp morning, Orrin stepped out the door of their farmhouse to find two strangers on horseback dragging something behind them. As the duo approached, he caught sight of the glint of Silver Stars on both of their vests. These were Deputy Marshals approaching his home. One of the riders seemed to be a woman.

Bennett and Lydia rode up to the farmer and Bennett spoke, "I'm Deputy U.S. Marshal Bennett and this young lady is my partner, Marshal Forsyth. We need water for our mounts. We would also require the renting of a small wagon if you have one, to transport the deceased person that we are dragging behind us. I am prepared to write a script to you for up to twenty-five dollars for this urgent mission."

Orrin quickly accepted, "Twenty-five dollars is a lot of money. Yes! We will do it." Then, remembering his manners, "but first, have you two had breakfast yet? My wife, Cassie, would love some company and I might add that she's a very fine cook."

Cassie came to the porch at the sound of conversation and smiled at her guests. The whiff of bacon frying caught their attention and the two of them conjured up a breakfast by a Texas farmer's wife. It was an invitation they could not refuse.

Cassie indeed proved herself a good cook. Breakfast was crisp bacon, two fried eggs cooked the way that each person liked them. Buttermilk biscuits with a homemade blackberry jam rounded out the meal. Coffee was rich and dark, just the way that frontier families liked it.

After the meal, in spite of Cassie's protests, Lydia helped Cassie wash, dry, and put away her dishes and cooking utensils. Cassie changed into her market day's outfit and prepared to take the reins of her personal farm wagon.

Bennett and Lydia performed the honors of loading the deceased into the bed of her wagon and tied it down with ropes to the wagon bed. Orrin hitched up Cassie's team to the wagon and helped her to the driver seat. Orrin mounted his own saddle horse.

When all was ready, Bennett gave the signal to move out at a walk. The small parade proceeded slowly eastward down the Sherman Road toward Paris.

Around two hours later, the group entered the town square and headed to the funeral parlor. While Lydia and the farm couple held at the funeral yard gates, Bennett entered the main doors to explain the situation to the undertaker.

A few minutes later, the gates opened and Cassie drove the small wagon into the yard and, like an expert farm-bred girl, backed her wagon to the loading door of the parlor and waited patiently while the undertaker's helpers unloaded their cargo.

After accomplishing that essential task, Orrin and Cassie accompanied Bennett and Lydia to the courthouse where Cassie waited at the wagon hitching post while Orrin walked into the courthouse to the District U.S. Marshal's office with the two deputies.

Deputy Bennett explained to Roseanne the transaction of the wagon rental to transport a murder victim and she paid the twenty-five dollars in exchange for the promissory script. Orrin left the Marshal's office with a smile and money in his pocket. He was a happy man indeed. He felt good. He and Cassie had aided the law and still made a few dollars for their service.

Bennett and Lydia entered Marshal Franklin's office and apprised him of the circumstances. Franklin thought for only a minute before issuing the following instructions, "Bennett, Forsyth, I want you to get Deputy Marshal Seth Grimes and the three of you will return to that cabin site and do as the escapee did. That is, you enter the river at the point that he did, and get to the other side. When you climb out, check for sign and follow it. We now know that he is in the Territory. You see if you can track him to wherever he might be. You have one week. If you can find him, bring him back here one way or another. That is, handcuffed to the saddle or over it! I want that man!"

Well, there it was! Lydia was finally entering the Indian Territory as a Deputy United States Marshal. Her thoughts reflected on a statement that Bass Reeves had made to her a few weeks earlier, "Go in disguise, and carry a good rifle. I suggest a Winchester. You might just need it."

CHAPTER ELEVEN

GABE JOHNSON

The following morning, Lydia rendezvoused with Deputy Marshals Bennett, and Grimes in front of the Lamar County Courthouse. She was definitely dressed for a ride in the Indian Territory. In fact, from a distance, Lydia could pass for a young man on a horse.

The two men were surprised by her attire but appreciated the wisdom of her disguise. She had dressed to carry out her duties as Deputy U.S. Marshal

Deputy Grimes, Lydia found out by conversation with him and Bennett, had been selected by Marshal Franklin to accompany them because he was a seasoned law officer as well as an expert tracker.

Lydia opted for attire conforming to Bass Reeves' suggestion in that she wore dark colored men's trousers tucked into her calf high riding boots with spurs. She wore dark brown suspenders over a medium gray shirt. Her cartridge belt was slung comfortably around her waist and she sported her Colt .44. She had pinned up her hair under her dark gray cowboy hat. The dark blue and white polka dot silk bandana lay loosely tied around her neck. The Silver Star shined brightly on her shirtfront.

Also suggested by Deputy Marshal Reeves, Lydia had stopped by the local jail and borrowed a Winchester rifle from the Paris Sheriff's office. She surprised Deputy John Lang when she demonstrated her knowledge of operating a lever action rifle. She selected one that she felt was appropriate for her use, inspected it for cleanliness, and smooth operation of the lever and mechanism.

She also selected a box of the correct caliber ammunition. After her departure, Deputy Lang just smiled and shook his head. That new Lady Marshal was something else. She would make some man a good wife.

Going on mid-morning the Marshal trio approached Elliott's cabin along the Red River. They sat their horses and surveyed the scorched earth remains from the brush fire started by the escaping Gabe Johnson.

Slowly, they moved forward on horseback toward the riverbank. Their eyes constantly moved, searching the ground for whatever clue they could find that might reveal more about their fugitive.

At the river's edge, they stopped astounded. Looking across the Red River, they quickly determined that no horse could have climbed out over that steep embankment facing them.

Bennett and Grimes questioned aloud their own reasoning about direction the fugitive swam his mount to climb out on the other side of the river.

Lydia contemplated the situation and injected her own thoughts, "What if—what if, he never climbed out across the river, but went upstream and came out again on the Texas side? Think about it. If he had gone down stream, he would have come out closer to Paris, which was getting too hot for him. Going up stream, he would be more confident of escaping the law. He might even have taken the ferry at Garrett's Bluff across the Red."

Her reasoning struck both of her partner Marshals into thought. After a few minutes, Bennett turned to Grimes, "You lead out, Seth. You're the tracker. We'll follow your thoughts and experience.

Seth led out northwest along the Red, his eyes ever alert to the embankments of the river. Within a mile, he suddenly drew up his horse and dismounted to more carefully inspect the ground.

After several minutes, he turned to Bennett and Lydia, "Well, Lydia. I hate to admit it, but you're correct. The SOB climbed out of the river right there." He pointed to the embankment and all saw the deep indentations of a struggling horse climbing out of the river. Tracks were deep in the soft earth at that point and led off toward the Sherman Road.

They followed hoof prints that lengthened in stride after a few minutes, and then, inexplicitly the tracks turned back toward Paris. Grimes clenched his teeth at what he read in the turn. "This guy is definitely either bold or quite insane. He knows that there are Deputy Marshals on his back and yet he continues to challenge us to a game of Catch Me if You Can."

Bennett could only say one thing, "Damn! He could just as well as have ambushed us on the return trip to town!"

Grimes instantly agreed with him. "I wonder if you two preceded him down the road. That may have happened."

Lydia was deep in thought. Suddenly, she spoke up, "I have a bad feeling. We need to get to the Waters Farm as quickly as possible."

Bennett looked at Lydia, "Do you suppose?"

Lydia answered him directly, "I don't know, but they went to town with us and by the time they must've arrived back home? I hate to think about it further. This man is definitely a twisted mind. Nothing he does would surprise me at this point. I only know that I have bad feelings about that farm."

Grimes listened to the conversation and remarked, "I think Lydia's right. We need to ride hard and fast."

At his last comment, the three law officers as one put spurs to their mounts and streamed down the Sherman Road toward the turn off to the Water's farm.

Within the hour, the three marshals turned off toward the farm, and when about half a mile from it, Bennett turned to Lydia and directed, "Lydia, I want you to ride as fast as you can about a hundred yards to the right and then turn towards the farm. Seth and I will approach straight on to the farmhouse. I want an edge if your thoughts are true. You have only a few minutes to get where you should be."

Lydia clucked to Chester as she put a spur to his right side and he responded. When she touched both spurs to his flanks, he burst into an all out run to the right side of the farm. Lydia, now accustomed to his gait, leaned into the spirit of the ride.

Bennett and Grimes dismounted and each drew out a cigarette and smoked it quickly, giving Lydia time to get into position. They looked into each other's eyes and knew what they must do. They nodded and ground out their tobaccos and remounted. Several minutes later, they rode into the farmyard.

The two deputies dismounted at the water trough. At that moment, the front door of the house opened, and Orrin Waters emerged walking toward them. He stopped within fifteen feet of them and said, "Welcome to my farm. You are welcome to water your animals." He appeared quite distressed.

Bennett scanned Orrin's face and read his eyes. He suddenly knew the situation. Someone was holding his wife Cassie as hostage so that he would do as ordered.

He asked Orrin directly in low tones, "Is there someone inside the house with Cassie?" to which Orrin could only acknowledge with his eyes. He kept eyeing towards the right of his face.

Bennett definitely knew the situation. He lowered his head and remarked to Deputy Grimes, "Our game has got the wife."

Suddenly, the door of the farmhouse burst open and Gabe Johnson exited with Cassie in front of him with right arm held firmly behind her in an arm lock. He screamed out, "I got you now, you Marshals. Raise your hands, lawmen, and keep them high. I'm going to be more famous than Billy the Kid.

The two lawmen complied with his demand.

Gabe continued, "I kilt me eight others before, but now, I'm going to kill me two Marshals and this farmer family. Prepare to meet your Maker!"

Lydia had ridden Chester as fast and as hard as she could. She stopped now on the right side of the farmhouse when she heard Gabe's initial challenge. She dismounted quickly and dropped Chester's reins, moving forward with the Winchester in hand. She worked the lever as silently as possible and readied for action.

Rounding the building, she saw Gabe had his back to her and she immediately assessed the situation. She shouldered the rifle and waited long minutes, hoping for a quick opening to act. She thought, "Keep him talking Bennett, keep him talking."

At that time, Gabe Johnson delivered his most chilling statement, "Go to Hell, Marshals."

He threw Cassie to the ground and with wild eyes coupled with insane laughing threw his revolver straight out in front of him to point at her two partners.

Lydia yelled out "Federal Officer," and distracted Gabe for a split second. He turned quickly and fired a round in her direction. The slug whined past Lydia's side, and she simultaneously squeezed off her first round. Marshals Bennett and Grimes drew their revolvers and fired.

In the next instant, Gabe Johnson lurched upward with the smack of a .44-40 slug imbedded in his chest. His own revolver fired into the ground as two more bullets hit him high in the back almost at the same time.

At the same instant, the Lady Marshal's rifle cracked again and Johnson jerked backward to fall directly onto the ground. His right hand twitched in an attempt to cock his revolver and shoot again.

Orrin Waters ran to Cassie, knelt down and tenderly took her into his arms and hugged her lovingly. They both cried tears of relief and each kissed away the terror of earlier moments.

Lydia moved slowly forward, levering yet another round into the chamber, and held it at the ready. Bennett and Grimes also moved forward, revolvers at the ready. Gabe Johnson lay grotesquely still, the wild look of sheer insanity etched forever on his face.

Deputy Marshal Ross Bennett turned to look directly into Lydia's eyes. "Well, partner, you took your own sweet time in getting here. I thought sure Seth and I were goners."

Lydia gasped in disbelief, and, then, he broke into a wide grin, as did Grimes. Laughing, they both stepped forward then and shook Lydia's hand. Bennett complimented her, "You did good, Lydia!"

Deputy Grimes nodded his approval saying, "Lydia, you can side me anytime."

Lydia looked down upon the fallen killer and realized a disappointing fact. "This is not the man who murdered my friend, Annie and her family. This man is only about twenty-four years old."

The third man involved with the Schuler family murder was still at large.

She unchambered the round in her Winchester and turning toward the farm couple told them, "All is good now. We finally got this man." Then, she helped Orrin raise Cassie to her feet and hugged her. Lydia could feel the trembling body inside her arms, in spite of the fact that danger had ended.

Grimes turned to Orrin and inquired, "Where's this man's horse?"

Orrin pointed to his small stable to the left of the house. Seth walked that way exclaiming over his shoulder, "We'll take him out of here the way he came on to your farm. On his horse," he hesitated only a moment, continuing with "tied over the saddle."

Several minutes later, Bennett and Grimes slung the deceased outlaw over his saddle and roped him securely.

By that time, Lydia had tenderly helped Cassie into the house speaking in soft comforting tones. After a cup apiece of Cassie's hot coffee, the law trio mounted their horses. They waved farewell to the Waters couple and began their trek back to Paris.

They would go first to the undertaker, and then, to report the demise of the wanted man to the sheriff's office and to United States Marshal Franklin.

Bennett and Lydia rode ahead side-by-side while Grimes led the burdened saddle horse.

CHAPTER TWELVE

LYDIA'S REWARD

After depositing the wanted murderer Gabe Johnson's remains with the undertaker, the three Marshals reported to Marshal Franklin on the results of their journey. After hearing their reports, he nodded affirmatively, congratulated them, and informed them announced that there was no federal bounty on the deceased.

He thought for a moment and then with a grin on his face related that Lamar County had put a $500 bounty on the deceased and that if they pressed the sheriff's office, the three of them could collect <u>that</u> reward.

Franklin nodded his head and agreed, "Lydia—Marshal Forsyth, I think you have earned the right to enter the Indian Territory with a party of Marshals on a warrant expedition. In any case, I would expect that you three should take a few days off and report for your next assignment on Friday morning."

The three compadres left the District U.S. Marshal's Office with grins on their faces. Seth Grimes announced, "I'm going to spend the next few days with my family, maybe take them on a picnic if that was what his wife wanted."

Ross Bennett related, "I'll probably just hang around town and maybe have a few beers at a local saloon."

They turned to Lydia and inquired as to her thoughts and plans for the next two days. Lydia thought a few seconds, then, divulged, "Perhaps I will work with Chester a bit. I want to train him to do a few more actions that I might need while riding the Territory."

Her partners thought that was a good idea.

Before the trio disbanded for the short break in service, they entered the Lamar County Sheriff's office and found Sheriff Theodore Walker sitting behind his oaken desk. He looked up as the three Marshals entered and rose to greet them.

"I have been to the undertaker. Can I presume that you are here to inquire and collect the Lamar County reward for this wanted man?"

Seth Grimes spoke up, "You can bet your last dollar that's why we're here." Bennett and Forsyth nodded in agreement.

Theodore hemmed and hawed for a few moments before replying, "Well, considering that you are officers of the law, you're not qualified for this reward."

Seth immediately corrected him, "Correction! We are not allowed to collect Federal rewards, we ARE authorized to collect other than federal rewards. We want nothing more than what is fair. Divide that reward by three and give us our due."

Lydia interrupted the conversation, "Three days ago, I borrowed this Winchester Rifle from your office. I dispatched the killer with this rifle. I'd like to keep it. I'll accept this rifle as payment in full for my part of the reward."

Sheriff Walker without hesitation nodded his head and announced, "Take the rifle. It's yours now."

Afterwards, he opened his safe and handed over two thirds of the reward money to Grimes and Bennett. All were satisfied with the arrangement.

Outside the sheriff's office, the three deputies bid a quick farewell to each other. Grimes mounted his horse and rode off toward his home. Bennett took his mount and led it by the reins to the livery stable before heading to the nearest saloon.

Lydia climbed into the saddle and spoke softly to the bay. "Let's go for a ride, Chester. There are some moves I want you to do." She turned him toward the west end of town and trotted out onto the prairie.

Lydia had been working with Chester in his livery stable corral in her spare time. Joe Martin, the livery owner, observed her a few times as she took Chester to the center of the corral and then, she reached down and picked up his left front hoof, gently pulling his leg back. She seemed intent on teaching him to bow.

Martin wondered, "Now, just what would she do that for? I've never seen anyone train a horse to do that before." Around the stable, conversation with other riders tossed around ideas about the Lady Deputy Marshal's unusual training techniques.

After several patient hours, Lydia got to the point where the horse would bow with both legs.

Finally, the time arrived to test Chester on her true intentions. Once out on the lonesome land, Lydia walked her horse for a short time. Then, she suddenly spurred the bay into a hard run. Chester stretched out into a ground-eating run and seemed to enjoy it. Lydia leaned forward against the animal's neck and urged him onward.

After several long minutes with the wind in her face, she reined him quickly in. Chester skidded to a dust-swirling halt and Lydia leaped out of the saddle. Holding the reins firmly in her hand, she leaned down to firmly pat the bay on his upper left front leg, while repeating the words "Down, Chester. Down, Chester."

Chester stood looking at her as if she had lost her mind. A few moments went by and Lydia remounted to once again, spur the animal into a fast run. Again, she reined in firmly and Chester slid to an abrupt halt. She jumped out of the saddle to repeat her earlier coaxing.

This time, Chester understood what his mistress wanted, and he knelt down on his front legs and then turned to lie down on his side on the prairie. Lydia praised the bay and stroked his face and neck, until suddenly, she climbed onto Chester's back and firmly stated, "Up, Chester. Let's run!"

Moments later, the two were again streaming across the empty prairie. Lydia repeated this exercise with Chester several times and each time, the horse responded well to his mistress.

Lydia once more swung into the saddle and spurred the animal to a fast run, after a long five minutes, she sawed back on the reins and when Chester slid to a dust-swirling halt, she grabbed the Winchester from the saddle boot and the horse went down into the bow and rolled over to lay still.

Lydia leaned her rifle across the saddle and with empty Winchester, worked the lever action three or four times, pulling the trigger and listening to the audible metallic clicks. Chester never flinched. He had experienced gunfire with this lady before.

In the next moment, she grabbed the reins and swung her right leg over the saddle, yelling, "Chester! Let's go!" The animal rose up with Lydia on his back. She spurred him into another run and at the same time slid the rifle back into the scabbard.

After several minutes, Lydia reined him again, and this time, she dismounted and spent considerable time softly speaking to the animal and stroking his face, neck, and shoulders. "I knew you could do it. You are a smart horse and I love you for it."

After a long time praising her horse, she remounted and walked the gelding to the edge of Paris, Texas and then lightly stroked Chester's flanks with her spurs. They trotted smartly through the town square where a few spring wagons holding farm produce waited for customers. She tied Chester to the nearest hitching post at the boardwalk.

As usual, the vendors seemed to be mainly ladies who had their own gardens and wished to gather a few dollars to help support their families.

Lydia surveyed all of the produce and returned to one in particular. A young woman with two blonde-haired children stood anxiously beside her wagon. Lydia inquired, "What's your name? Are you here every Saturday?"

The young blonde blue-eyed woman answered, "My name's Emily and these are my children who like to help in my garden. My daughter is Hanna, after her grandmother, and my son is Joseph, after his father. May I help you with a selection?"

Lydia smiled at the woman and answered, "Yes. As a matter of fact, I think I would love some of your nicest carrots for my horse. He has performed well today and he deserves a treat. I would like a small bunch. What is the charge?"

Emily responded, and Lydia produced a $1 bill. The cost was less, but she accepted the small bunch of robust carrots and waved off any change. She responded by saying, "Small children need a sweet treat now and then. Buy them a peppermint stick or so."

She left Emily and the celebrating children to return to Chester who was enjoying a well-deserved drink at the watering trough.

After remounting, Lydia guided Chester to Martin's Livery Stable where she walked him to his stall, rubbed him down with burlap bags, forked a measure of hay into his feeder and laced it with a handful of grain. Then, she plucked off a large carrot and holding his head by the bridle, fed him his first treat. She stroked his neck while he munched away on his carrot. Lydia fed him one more and then slipped out, leaving Chester to the stable boy to further care for him.

Back at the Peterson Hotel, Lydia changed into city clothes without her Star and gun belt. She visited the café for a small supper of fried chicken, biscuits, and garden salad. Her waitress friend, Helen Waters took a break to sit with her. She inquired about Lydia's health and her Paris childhood.

After her meal, she retired to her room. She washed up in the porcelain basin with pitcher water and scented homemade soap, then shucked her clothes and donned her nightgown. She slipped into bed, and when her head touched the pillow, once again she began to dream of days long past.

CHAPTER THIRTEEN

VISIONS OF EARLY LIFE

Lydia felt bone tired when she slipped into her bed. She turned down the oil lamp and closed her eyes looking forward to a good night's rest. Try as she might, she could not shut down the consistent reminiscing of her subconscious.

Visions of her early life were quite vivid as her mind moved slowly to revive events that shaped her into the woman that she had become.

Eight years previous, Laura Forsyth knelt tending her flower garden along the front of their home. Her daughter, thirteen-year old Lydia, was at school and her husband Jonathan was at his job in downtown Paris, Texas.

Laura held her favorite hand hoe, on her hands and knees weeding out her garden. The vibrations of her movements and rigorous thrusts into the soil irritated an unseen diamond back rattlesnake six feet away. It lay hidden under numerous spring blooms so that she never noticed it.

The large snake coiled silently in the shade of the blooms and when its diamond shaped head rose above the coil, its rattles vibrated vigorously. Laura turned suddenly to come face to face with the deadly reptile. A split second later, the snake struck its full length to sink fangs into her throat.

She instinctively grabbed out with her left hand while still holding the hand hoe in her right. She squeezed and tugged hard at the snake while the venom surged into her body. After a mighty pull, she managed to dislodge the snake from her throat and slam it on to the soil. With all her remaining strength, she struck the wildly thrashing snake with her hand hoe until she severed the head from the body.

Laura immediately felt nauseous and weak. She could hardly move. She screamed out, as loud as she could, and then, fainted forward into her precious flowers. Her body seemed uncontrollable as she attempted to call out again and again. Her body jerked with the poison raging through her blood stream.

Katherine Sterns, her neighbor, heard Laura's first cries and dashed out of her door to see her friend on the ground, her body seizing in wild movements. She rushed out her front gate and into the Forsyth's yard to reach Laura and take her into her arms.

She looked into Laura's eyes and saw the pain and when she lowered her eyes to understand her friend's dilemma, she saw two fang marks on Laura's throat. Then, she saw the large decapitated rattlesnake and understood the dire situation.

Katherine held Laura tenderly in her arms as the stricken woman gasped for breath and, a moment later, closed her eyes and slumped limply against her bosom.

Katherine hoarsely breathed out, "Oh my God! Laura's dead. How can I ever tell Jonathan and their daughter Lydia about this?" She couldn't contain herself any longer; she shrieked loudly and suddenly neighbors from all sides of the dirt street came rushing to her aid.

There was nothing so many neighbors could do for Laura; the snakebite was too lethal for her heart.

Lenora Walker was one of the first to arrive on the scene to Katherine's call. She quickly took in the situation and speaking rapidly, uttered, "Someone has got to ride to the square and tell Jonathan! I got to get him here! He must be here quickly. I'll get my horse and summon him directly!"

The others kneeling beside Laura could only nod.

Lenora turned and rushed out the gate to the small stable behind her home and not taking time to saddle her steel gray mare, slipped a bridle in place and hiking up her skirts, leaped astride her mount and turned it toward the middle of town and Jonathan's office.

Jonathan Forsyth sat in his office speaking to a new customer when Lenora Walker slid her mare to the hitching rack immediately outside his office. Her mount had scarcely stopped when she did a flying dismount and rushed to his office door pounding on it and yelling out with such urgency that Jonathan jumped up and rushed to see what the commotion was all about.

Lenora breathlessly babbled out, "Jonathan, you must come quick!" Laura has been snake bit and, I'm afraid, has died. We need you immediately!"

Forgetting his customer, Jonathan yelled out, "I'm on my way!" He ran out the back of his office to the lean-to shed and grabbed up his own horse. He gripped the saddle horn and, shoving his boot into the left stirrup, he slung himself up into the saddle and galloped the entire distance to his home to find over a dozen neighbors gathered around the west side of Laura's flower garden.

He dismounted quickly, not caring to tie his mount to the hitching rack and rushed to his wife. Katherine still held the stricken woman in her arms. Seeing Jonathan, she silently passed Laura unto his arms with soft words, "I was first here. I could do nothing to help her. She passed in my arms."

Jonathan could do nothing more but to nod his understanding and hold Laura to his breast as tears of sorrow flooded his eyes. His only thought at this moment, "How will I tell Lydia of this? How do you tell a thirteen year old girl that her mother has died from a snake bite?"

A sympathetic hand lightly touched Jonathan's shoulder and he turned his tear-stained face to peer into the understanding eyes of Reverend Louis Michaels, his pastor.

Another neighbor and congregation member had rushed to notify the minister of the trouble. Reverend Michaels had also dropped what he was doing and rushed to the scene.

Jonathan could only hold his stricken wife in his arms and ask of the minister, "Why?"

Reverend Michaels answered in the only way that he could at that moment, "The Lord has need of Laura with his angels. Rest assured that she sleeps in the arms of God."

Jonathan looked down and suddenly saw the body of the snake. He became highly distraught, sobbing and gently handed Laura to his Pastor. He grabbed up the hand hoe that Laura used and viciously attacked the dead reptile effectively chopping it the length of it into a dozen pieces.

Some of the women shrank back from this uncharacteristic violence, but the men present understood his actions.

Afterward, he dropped the tool and with head in his hands sobbed out his heart felt sorrow. Neighbors stood in silence for several long minutes until Jonathan regained his composure and turned to his minister with the words, "Please help me get her inside and stay with her. I need to get Lydia from school. She needs to be here also."

After Jonathan and Reverend Michaels carried Laura into the house and laid her gently on their bed, the pastor knelt beside her and began to pray for Jonathan and Lydia.

Jonathan exited the house and moved through his front gate, attempting to mount his horse. His frustration was such that the animal shied away from him. He stopped for a long moment, and lowered his head in prayer. When he again looked up, he softly spoke to his horse, "Gallant, I need you for an important ride. We need to get Lydia."

The animal understood the name Lydia and when Jonathan reached slowly for the reins, the gelding moved toward him. Jonathan mounted and slowly rode towards the school where unsuspecting Lydia was engaged in her lessons. He had to gather his thoughts before he saw his daughter.

Long minutes later, Jonathan arrived at the school. He somberly dismounted and looped the reins of his horse around the hitching post in front of the building.

He paused several minutes thinking over and over in his mind how he would tell Lydia of her mother's passing. One thing was sure, the two of them loved each other and would support each other.

Jonathan entered the schoolhouse and paused in the entrance. Teacher, Miss Jean Malone, looked up at him while reading from a book. Jonathan motioned for her to join him so Jean read for a few moments longer and then rose from her desk to address a fair-haired girl on the front row, "Rachel, please read the next page aloud to the class."

Jean moved silently to Jonathan with questioning eyes. Jonathan motioned for a private talk and they moved toward the door of the schoolhouse. With barely audible whispers, he told Jean Malone, "There's been a terrible accident at home and I must take Lydia there at once. I can tell you no more at this time."

Jean evaluated the distress on his face and nodded her understanding. She motioned for him to step outside onto the steps and that she would be back directly.

A few minutes passed and the door opened to exit Miss Malone and Lydia who held a puzzled look on her face. She was surprised to see her father waiting for her.

At this point, Lydia's imagined memories ended and her actual memories began.

Jonathan thanked the teacher and she retreated into the building. Jonathan took Lydia aside and bid her to follow him. Ironically, he led to the very picnic table in the schoolyard that Lydia had bid farewell to her best friend Annie two years earlier.

"Please sit down with me, Lydia. I have something of the utmost importance to tell you."

Lydia looked deeply into her father's eyes, and immediately, she somehow knew, "It's Mother! Isn't it? There's something wrong with Mother. Tell me Father! Tell me now. I need to know."

Jonathan swallowed hard and hung his head for a moment or two before answering, "Lydia, there's been a terrible accident at home. A rattlesnake. I'm afraid that I have to tell you that your mother Laura is dead."

Lydia sat stunned for a long minute. She searched her father's eyes intensely and saw the devastation in them. She spoke slowly and directly, "I want to see her. I need to see my mother right now."

Jonathan could only nod his head. Standing, he took her hand and led her to his horse. Jonathan mounted and offered his left hand down to Lydia. She accepted and he swung her up on the animal behind him. He turned the steel gray toward home. Lydia put her arms around her father's waist and hung on for dear life as he urged his mount forward. She wept into the back of her father's coat as Gallant carried them home.

Friends and neighbors had gathered around the Forsyth house to express condolences to the family. Jonathan drew Gallant to the hitching post in front of his gate and allowed Lydia to dismount before him. The two of them walked solemnly to the door and entered. The small crowd stood in silence.

Jonathan motioned for Lydia to follow him to the bedroom where Laura lay reposed in peaceful eternal slumber. The reverend had closed her eyes and positioned her to appear serene in her viewing state.

When Lydia approached the bed, Reverend Michaels stood up from the bedside chair and moved away in respect for the young daughter. Jonathan stood beside the pastor with his head hung in silent prayer for his beloved wife.

Lydia looked down upon her mother; she reached out and lightly touched her cheeks. They seemed cool to her, not warm like when she kissed her mother farewell before leaving for school that morning.

The girl's eyes filled with tears as she bent and kissed the cool cheek of her departed best friend. And then, she bent forward and lay her head against her mother's breast and held her cool hand in hers as she shed more tears in silent weeping for her second great loss within two years.

Four days later, Lydia stood in silence with her father and friends at the Paris, Texas cemetery and watched as Reverend Michaels conducted final rites for her precious mother. Lydia held tightly to Jonathan's hand as the pastor concluded the solemn ceremony and bid her and her father to approach the grave.

The undertaker's men lowered the coffin into the ground, and before the first shovel of dirt was laid into the grave, Lydia took a bouquet of favorite wild flowers that she had picked from her mother's garden and dropped them carefully on top of the coffin. Jonathan did likewise.

Long minutes later, the grave was sealed and Lydia with Jonathan turned to face the onlookers to accept their humble wishes of condolence on their tragic loss.

Father and daughter remained until the very end of the funeral.

Finally, they were the only two left to stand and gaze at the fresh mound with a temporary wooden cross. A carved stone marker had been ordered and would replace the cross in due time. Silence hung over both of them.

A few minutes later, Lydia spoke her first words since morning. "Father, before we leave, I need to visit a friend who stays here. Please give me a few minutes alone with my friend, Annie."

Jonathan understood only too well. He nodded to her. He walked to the cemetery entrance and stood there in prayer while Lydia moved off to another section and her friend.

Fifteen or so minutes later, Lydia approached and took Jonathan's hand. Together, they walked to their waiting carriage and rode to their home.

A few months later, after school let out for the summer, Jonathan knew that it was time to make his rounds to the various general stores and trading posts in the Indian Territory that carried his company's wares. He decided to have Lydia stay with a neighbor family while he made his business rounds.

Prior to finalizing his plans, he sat with Lydia at their kitchen table sipping coffee. She sipped a cup of her mother's favorite tea with a spoon of honey added for sweetness. He expressed his thoughts about his plans.

"Lydia, I need to make my semi-annual trip into the Territory for business. I'll arrange for you to stay here in Paris with Mr. and Mrs. Howard and their children. You know them and their daughter. Janet is a friend of yours. I should not be gone more than two weeks. I know that they'll take good care of you and you should have good times with them."

Lydia went silent and bowed her head for a few minutes while Jonathan searched her eyes for her thoughts when she looked up. Finally, she spoke, "Father, I want to go with you. I know that the Territory is fraught with danger, but after all, you taught me how to shoot and bought me my own revolver. I could cut my hair shorter and dress like a boy. I shall have it no other way. I can't bear to be without you, even for two weeks. My mind is made up and I can be just as stubborn as you because I am your daughter."

"Lydia!" Jonathan had never expected her reaction.

"No, Father, I won't take no for an answer. I'm determined to be at your side on your trip into the Indian Territory. When do we leave?"

Well, who could argue with that? Jonathan took a very deep breath and thought out the circumstances. At long last, he very reluctantly agreed that Lydia would accompany him on his trip.

He replied as such, "Against my better judgment, you may just be right. All right, cut your hair shorter like a boy. We'll obtain some boy clothing at the clothing store along with some shoes and especially a hat. You need to wear a hat, maybe a cowboy style hat to help shade your face to onlookers. But, as you wish, you will be with me as we travel the scenic territory."

True to his word, two early mornings later Jonathan hitched up Gallant to his small one horse buggy and loaded his sample case and box business catalogs into the boot of the wagon. He then loaded their travel duffels stocked with extra clothes and personal items into the boot as well.

Jonathan Forsyth wore his travel outfit of dark trousers tucked into calf high leather boots, light gray shirt open at the collar, and a dusty dark blue floppy slouch hat pulled down in front to shield his eyes from the sun. A cartridge belt was buckled around his waist along with holster and a Colt .44 Frontier. Next to his left side sat his single barrel lever action shotgun. A box of ammunition lay within easy reach.

Lydia's usually long dark hair was cropped to neck length. She wore dark charcoal boy's trousers with suspenders and boy style leather shoes. She had a light blue baggy shirt buttoned at the collar, and wore a dark gray floppy cowboy-style hat, to also shield her face from the sun. She wore a belt around her waist with small holster that carried her personal revolver.

Within an hour after sunrise, Jonathan and Lydia boarded his wagon and set out for a three-week sales circuit into the Indian Territory. He turned to his daughter and asked, "Well, what should your name be for this journey?"

Lydia thought for a bit before replying, "I like the name Danny. Yes! Call me Danny, Father."

He grinned at his new son, "Danny it is then. When in public you answer to the name Danny."

Then, Jonathan surprised Lydia when he turned the wagon down the trail out of Paris toward the east instead of toward the west and Garrett's Bluff Ferry operations.

She mentioned it at once, "Father, I thought we had to travel to Garrett's Bluff to cross the river into the Territory."

He replied in soft voice, "My dear daughter, my company has made special arrangements so that I may cross on the steamboat at Pine Bluff Boat Landing. You have never been on a steamboat, so this should be an experience for you." Lydia immediately smiled with excitement.

Once at Pine Bluff boat docks, she sat in the wagon while Jonathan met with the boarding authority. He presented his papers with special passage and the authority logged him and Lydia along with the horse and buggy onto the loading sequence.

People in the general area did not seem to take special notice of Lydia. They indeed mistook her for a teen-aged boy.

Finally, they were called to board the steamboat. Their position was such that they would be the first and only commodity to be off loaded on the opposite shore. Thirty minutes later, the steamboat fired up furnaces and chugged out of the port to chug to the left and cross the Red River.

The boat eased up to the wooden dock on the opposite side of the Red and quickly off loaded Jonathan and his party. With such a short journey, Jonathan and "Danny" had avoided casual conversation and questions from other travelers.

The steamboat then surged forward back into the stream of the Red River and began its journey down stream into the Trinity River to the waiting cotton markets in the Dallas area.

Jonathan and Lydia were suddenly alone on the dock as they prepared to travel into the Territory. Jonathan turned to his daughter and stated, "Well, Daughter. You are now in the Indian Territory. We have a long journey to make. We'll camp tonight at a place that I know of about twenty some miles north of here. Are you ready?"

Lydia turned to smile at her father and nodded her head to say, "Yes! Let's go. I want to see everything that you do and where you have traveled in your business."

Jonathan grinned at her and slapped the reins to his horse Gallant. They were off into the wilds of the Choctaw Nation.

That evening close to sundown, Jonathan slowed his rig and guided Gallant off the trail into a thick stand of closely grown trees and heavy brush. He continued until they were unseen from the trail above them and Lydia heard the quiet babble of a small stream.

Jonathan eased up on the reins and his horse stopped. He climbed out of the wagon and began unhitching Gallant from the wagon. Lydia looked around and within a few yards to the side was a closed circle of large rocks that formed a campfire ring. Other travelers had often used this site in times past. She dismounted to help her father unload their immediate camp needs.

Jonathan then got a bucket from a hook on the underside of his wagon and handed it to Lydia. "Go to the creek below and bring some water for Gallant."

Jonathan picketed his animal within some tall grasses, and while his daughter filled the water bucket, he went on to forage for dry tinder and kindling with which to start a small fire for supper and hot beverages.

Lydia found the stream and filled the bucket. She sipped a bit of the water from her cupped hand and found it quite refreshing. She listened carefully. The sun slowly disappeared in the west and she heard the soft splashes of fish in the center of the creek. She listened even more closely and heard the soft croaking of frogs along the water. She nodded to herself. She liked this small place of nature.

After bedrolls were arranged around the small campfire, Jonathan asked Lydia if she would like some fresh fish for supper. She immediately replied that she would.

"Well, then," said Jonathan, "out here in the Territory, there is no market. We'll have to fish for our supper."

He produced two fishing lines with small lead weights and hooks on the ends. He handed one to Lydia and she just stood there with it in her hand looking at it wondering what to do.

He went to the wagon and produced a small shovel with which he moved to the embankment and proceeded to dig up the ground. Presently, he pulled up half a dozen fat earthworms, which he placed on a white handkerchief.

He turned to Lydia and motioned for her to watch as he baited his hook for fishing. She watched intently and then she tried her hand at slipping a large earthworm onto her hook. She found satisfaction as she succeeded in this task. She watched as her father tossed his line as far into the center of the creek as he could. He then told Lydia to do the same and she did.

He instructed her on how to hold the line in her hand and to feel with the tip of her finger for little nibbles of a fish biting on the bait.

It wasn't long before both father and daughter felt the nibbles of fish on their bait and Jonathan jerked his line quickly setting the hook into the fish's mouth. He slowly coiled his line inward to shore to retrieve his prize.

Lydia mirrored her father and within minutes landed a slightly larger fish than her instructor who beamed with delight.

"Well," said Jonathan softly, "do you want to eat one fish or two?"

Lydia was beside herself with excitement. "I believe I could eat two such fish this evening."

The duo extracted their hooks from their catch, re-baited their hooks and cast once more into the depths of the stream. Within minutes, they had each caught another tasty fish.

Then, Jonathan explained and demonstrated how to clean their catch, and afterward took the entrails and tossed them into the water's edge. Jonathan explained, "We only take from nature what we need and then we give back. Sometime after dark, there will be various scavengers and other nocturnal creatures looking for a meal. They'll find our leavings and be thankful for them."

"What kind of creatures would come here, father?"

"There might just be coyote, eels, birds of prey such as owls, maybe a weasel or such. They will all be looking for a meal." Lydia nodded in understanding.

Then, Jonathan showed Lydia how to clean her two fish and debone them. After that, he cut some twigs with his sheath knife and stripped them of all foliage and branches to make a forked stick. He sharpened the forks with his knife and slid his fish onto the fork. Lydia did the same and they broiled their supper over the small fire.

After eating, they sat around the campfire and spoke in low tones about the land and about its possible inhabitants.

Finally, the moon was up and they readied for bed. Jonathan laid his shotgun next to him on the ground and, taking his revolver, slipped it under his pillow. He bid Lydia to do the same, saying, "Lydia, we are in a dangerous land. It'll get more dangerous the deeper we get into this territory. Do as I do, and be alert to all sounds out of the ordinary. Follow my lead always, and we will get through this travel safely. Good sleep to you, my dear daughter."

"Good night, Father. I love you."

Two days later, they entered the Choctaw Council area. Several of the tribe moved to meet them. Jonathan held his right hand up in peaceful greeting. He spoke slowly, "Halito, chim achukma?" meaning, "Hello, how are you?" His hand signal and verbal greeting were acknowledged, and returned. Many of the tribal council knew him and the why of his travels. They welcomed him into their camp.

Lydia was somewhat surprised that her father could speak in the Choctaw tongue. Little did she know at this time that she would acquire some of the language as well.

Jonathan dismounted from the buggy but bid Danny to remain seated on the wagon. "You can observe much from the high seat of a wagon. Look over the sights of the encampment."

Lydia felt a bit uneasy, but she obeyed her father and sat on the wagon, glancing around the area. She noticed Choctaw women and children eyeing her curiously and she smiled at them. She took note of the Indian girls in how they were dressed. For the most part the girls wore American style skirts and blouses. Some wore simple dresses that reminded her of the attire that she had worn while helping her mother tend to their garden in the back yard. Mother! Recognition of her loss took her breath.

The Choctaw boys appeared to be dressed much as she herself as a boy was attired. They stood in silence contemplating her. They also seemed curious about her.

Looking around the area, Lydia observed cultivated plots of land that resembled gardens. She suddenly realized that the Choctaw were a civilized nation of agriculture.

Momentarily, a young boy about her age approached the wagon and he raised his right hand saying the same phrase that Jonathan had used in greeting the elders. Lydia raised her hand also to return the greeting.

The boy then asked her in simple English, "What your name? I am called Shanafila, or Blue Hawk in your language."

Lydia nodded to the boy, "Hello, Blue Hawk. I am called, she started to say Lydia, but caught herself and stated Danny Forsyth. That is my father Jonathan who comes to offer trade goods for your trading post."

Blue Hawk nodded and turned back to his friends to rattle off a sentence of Choctaw, telling them of this newcomer. Blue Hawk then turned back to Lydia and with a smile announced, "I told them that you are our friend. We should get to know more of you while the elders do business. After you get a hut to stay in, we should meet and talk more."

For two days, Jonathan showed his company's tools and wares to the elders of the Choctaw Nation.

Finally, after a night of discussion, the elders told him their order for their trading post. He carefully wrote out the order and bid them to keep it in a safe place. The wares would be coming in by freight wagons out of Fort Smith within two weeks.

By this time, Lydia in the guise of Danny had made fast friends among the boys and girls of the tribe. She promised to return with her father on his next visit.

The following two weeks were an adventure for Lydia as Jonathan took her to several other trading posts and general stores in the Choctaw Nation. One of the highlights of her trip before returning to Paris was their stop at McAlester where she met James J. McAlester, the founder of the general store and of the town. She had a wonderful visit with Mrs. McAlester while Jonathan conducted his business with the prolific owner.

In the future, Lydia would make two more trips with Jonathan before being sent to Dallas to board and attend the Ladies Academy until graduation in June of 1890.

CHAPTER FOURTEEN

INTO THE NATIONS

It was Friday morning and Lydia awakened with the dawn as usual. She donned her robe and trekked to the bath area and her usual Friday tub of heated water. Although the water felt good to her, she could not linger.

Back in her room, she changed into her trail outfit of dark gray trousers with suspenders, light blue shirt buttoned to the collar, and calf high riding boots. She slung her cartridge belt around her waist and settled it for comfort, sliding her Colt .44 Frontier into the holster. She took up the Colt .41 Thunderer, and stuck it behind her waistband. Then, she loosely tied her dark blue and white polka dot bandana in place around her neck. The Silver Star glinted on her shirtfront.

Her duffle sat on the bed and she packed it with a couple of changes of clothing and her toiletries kit along with a towel and wash cloth. She felt that she had packed for at least a week in the wilds of the Territory.

Turning to the wooden closet, she retrieved a thigh length jacket, as she knew that it was cool in the evenings in the wilds.

Grabbing up her duffle and Winchester rifle, she left her room, spurs jingling all the way down to the lobby of the Peterson Hotel and out onto the street where she greeted Frank Sutton sitting in his horse taxi.

"Good morning, Frank. Please take me to the livery. I need to get Chester."

Frank returned her greeting, and once Lydia had tossed her duffle into the luggage bed and climbed onto the seat next to him with her Winchester and jacket, he lightly slapped the reins to his team and they made their way to the livery.

"Looks like you are going on a trip this morning, Lydia. Will you be gone long?"

"That depends on what happens in the Territory," remarked Lydia. "Hopefully it won't be too long."

Frank knew about the Deputies traveling into the Nations. It was dangerous business and sometimes it took a long time to find and apprehend those ruthless men for whom warrants had been issued.

At the livery, Lydia retrieved her duffle and waved farewell to Frank. She went to Chester who greeted her affectionately with a muzzle to her cheek, a horsey kiss if you will.

She stroked his face and spoke softly to him as she slipped his bridle on and opened the stall gate. Once outside, Chester figured that they were going for a ride. He stood still while she situated saddle blanket, saddle, and cinched him up. She then fastened her duffle to the saddle cantle and slipped the Winchester into the scabbard. They were ready.

Lydia led Chester out the livery door and mounted for an invigorating trot to the courthouse to meet with her fellow Deputies for this mission into the Territory. As she rode through the town square, various people turned to observe her. Some even waved greetings to her and she felt good. She smiled, especially when the children waved at her. She waved back.

At the courthouse, she looped Chester's reins around the hitching rack and let him take a drink from the water trough. Spurs jingled as she made her way to the District Marshal's office, and upon entering, Roseanne motioned her directly into Franklin's office.

Standing around the Marshal's desk were four men. Two of them, she already knew. They were Ross Bennett and Seth Grimes. The other two Deputies, she had not met yet. Marshal Bill Franklin introduced all to Lydia.

Bob Grant was in his thirties with dark eyes and hair. The lanky Deputy held out his hand to Lydia remarking, "I was on the other side of the square when you shot them bank robbers. Ross told me of your riding with him. I'm glad you are with us."

Lydia nodded as she shook his hand.

The fourth Deputy was an older, grim faced man named Jace Williams who scowled at her. He grumbled something incoherent under his breath but held out his hand to her. Lydia took it and it seemed overpowering, as if to demonstrate his strength. She held back a wince as she looked into his eyes and saw a definite dislike for her.

Franklin made mental note of Jace's dislike of Lydia before he told of the arrest warrant to be served. "Today, I have received a warrant for Luke Winters and four others reputed to be a gang of horse rustlers who take horses from Arkansas and Texas into the Territory and sell them. These men are dangerous in that some of them have murdered for the animals that they have stolen. Word has it that they use an old abandoned mustang ranch as their headquarters. Our informer states that it is within forty miles northeast of the Red within the Choctaw Nation."

Franklin then reached to his desk and produced a slightly crumpled piece of paper. He continued, "I have here a crudely drawn map of this rundown ranch location drawn by our *friend*. I have no idea of its accuracy, but I trust that Seth is capable of discerning the sketched landmarks.

You five are charged with serving this warrant and taking them. I trust that all of you will proceed with utmost caution."

An hour later, the five Deputies entered the Red River. Being August, the river level was low, and they walked their mounts directly across to the other side. Once out of the water, Lydia dismounted Chester and led him up the slight embankment as did the male members of her group.

Once on the opposite side of the river, they remounted. There was little conversation as each rode with their own thoughts as they entered the wilds of Choctaw Territory.

That night, the small posse of Deputies camped within eight miles of their intended destination. After hobbling their horses, they built a low campfire and laid out their bedrolls. Coffee was boiled and they partook of beef jerky and a handful of dried apple slices.

Looking ahead to an early morning start, they retired with one Deputy serving as guard and the others sleeping in four-hour watches. Lydia drew the first watch.

She sat a few feet beyond the glowing embers with a tree at her back, remembering her father, Jonathan's words, "A person who sits in the light of a campfire cannot see beyond the rim of his camp. You must always sit away in order to see and understand the night noises and movements."

Lydia felt, rather than heard, the slight scurries of tiny inhabitants of the land. A flutter of feathers from the opposite tree limbs brought the sight of a large owl seemingly looking inquisitively at her. Within moments, it gave its hooting call and flew with long wings flapping from the perch. She smiled with the sight of it.

Close to the end of her watch, she looked toward the horses. They seemed content to nibble morsels of fresh grasses, or lie down and roll around a bit. They did not seem alarmed in any way.

Finally, she awakened Seth for the second watch and went to her bedroll near the outskirt of the small campfire. After placing her Colt revolver under her pillow, it did not take long for her to slip off into a sound slumber, dreaming of fond memories.

It was nearing daybreak, when Ross Bennett knelt to awaken Lydia. She suddenly turned over and looked him straight in the eye. "I'm awake, Ross! I was just waiting for you to roust me out. The coffee already smells good. I'll be ready in a few minutes."

Lydia rose from her bedroll, took a few minutes to stretch her body and then, opening her canteen, poured some tepid water into a hand and lightly washed her face as it were. She then gathered up her bedroll and went to the horse grazing area. Chester was glad to see her. She poured another cupped hand of water and lifted it to the bay's muzzle. Moments later, she fastened her bedroll to the saddle cantle and was ready to ride. That is, she was ready to ride after a quick cup of strong campfire coffee.

Within the hour, the posse of five had doused their campfire with dirt and climbed into the saddle. Seth Grimes led out with the crumpled hand-drawn map at the ready.

Two hours later, they came to a small clearing where a hastily repaired corral held about twenty head of horses. Five sinister figures emerged from the run down cabin and were about to mount their animals.

Jace Williams took it upon himself to direct Bennett and Grimes to ride left some fifty yards and Lydia to ride to the right about fifty yards.

He and Bob Grant would ride directly down the center and challenge the suspected outlaws.

Bennett and Seth had barely reached their fifty-yard mark when the men at the corral were mounted and opened the gate for the stolen stock to be driven to their destination. Lydia was still on her way to her turn-around point.

Williams suddenly yelled out, "They are getting away! FEDERAL MARSHALS! Dismount and throw your hands up!"

One hundred yards or so separated the two factions. All at once, Williams and Grant spurred their mounts and charged directly toward the surprised men and their rustled stock.

The two Marshals met with immediate gunfire as the suspects drew revolvers or rifles and began an urgent charge of their own toward the pair of officers.

Bennett and Grimes turned sharply and rode directly toward the two left side rustlers, firing revolvers as they galloped forward. One rustler took a bullet in the left shoulder and grabbed the wound with his free arm. His horse began bucking in a circle and he was thrown to the ground to lie in pain until Grimes drew up to him and disarmed him.

Watching his partner fall wounded to the ground, the second outlaw on the far left turned his animal sharply around and spurred its flanks in a desperate attempt to flee the situation. Bennett fired two revolver shots at the escaping man but missed him.

The fugitive gained the protection of the forest edge and disappeared from sight. Bennett swore under his breath, "Damn it! I must be getting old. I should've had that guy!" He shook his head and reloaded his revolver as he joined Grimes with the wounded man.

Bob Grant rode steadily toward the center of the outlaw group firing his revolver. His mount was in mid-stride when the young law officer received a bullet in the chest. He threw up his arms and was flung backward off his horse to hit the ground rolling three times and then to lie still!

Williams fired his rifle on the run hitting one of the charging outlaws who immediately slumped over his mount and slowed it to a walk. The wounded man dropped from his horse to lie unmoving on the ground.

William's horse was in midstride when a rifle bullet slammed into its chest. It dived head first into the earth screaming as it fell dead and turned over, pinning Jace's left leg underneath.

The remaining outlaw was gutsy and rode rapidly toward him, firing his revolver again and again. He was intent on killing Williams.

Jace lost his rifle as his horse fell. He reached for his revolver and found that it had slipped out of his holster and lay just beyond his reach. Jace Williams knew then that he had only seconds to live.

At William's challenge and the resultant gunfire, Lydia turned Chester and spurred him into a life-or-death run toward the fallen men. She instinctively knew that Bob Grant was beyond help and she drove Chester toward Williams.

Reaching him, she yelled, "Stay down, Jace!"

Lydia quickly dismounted as Chester bowed on his front legs and rolled over. She immediately knelt behind him and lined her Colt directly on the rapidly approaching horseman.

Amid three shots fired by the outlaw from a galloping horse, and with bullets zipping and furrowing the ground around her, she shot him twice in the chest.

The rustler threw up his arms and toppled from his mount not five yards from her. Horses from the rustled stock streamed past her as she stood with revolver in hand behind her beloved horse. Chester had not been hit.

Jace Williams lay back on the ground breathing heavily. His eyes were wide with disbelief at the action that he had just witnessed.

Deputies Ross Bennett and Seth Grimes rode up to the scene with a prisoner in tow. Lydia stood over the man that Jace had shot and found that he was still alive. She insured that he was not armed, and then turned her attention to Williams who seemed unable to speak coherently.

Bennett and Grimes dismounted and stood for a long moment looking at Williams with grins on their faces. Williams looked up at them and the two friends immediately looked solemnly back at him.

Williams scowled a bit and grumbled, "Get this dead horse off me. I think my leg is broken."

Seth turned to Lydia "Get your lariat and rope this carcass. You drag it off. Bennett and I will lift and get Jace out."

Lydia got Chester up from his defensive position and taking her rope, dropped a noose around the dead animal's neck and mounted. "Say when ready!"

The two lawmen put their shoulders to the carcass and Seth called back, "Ready!"

Lydia and Chester dragged the carcass a few feet until Bennett called out, "We got him!"

She stopped Chester and retrieved her lariat from the broken animal. Dismounting, she moved to join her two companions in caring for the downed Deputy.

Bennett waved her off, "Fetch those wounded outlaws here and cuff them."

Lydia did as Ross Bennett bid her. Thirty minutes later, Lydia had the two wounded rustlers cuffed and sitting together a few yards from the fallen Deputy and his tenders. She observed that a few of the outlaws' saddled mounts had drifted back into the immediate area and she gathered them up to hobble them within close proximity to the group.

Finally, Jace Williams's leg was splinted and Seth handed over a small flask of whiskey to him as he made Jace ready to travel back to Paris.

Seth asked him the critical question, "Can you ride with your leg splinted like that? Keep in mind that it's going to be at least two days back to Paris. Can you make it riding? We've all got whiskey in our saddlebags. Call out when you need a pull."

Williams gritted his teeth and answered, "You just get me a horse and I'll mount it. I won't be carried back on a travois. That would be torture! I won't endure more pain than I have to. Bring me a horse and I'll try to mount with your help."

Seth volunteered, "Well, looks like you will ride my horse back to Paris. I'll ride one of the outlaws' animals with you in tow. Keep in mind that it is two days back to town, so we'll take it slow and easy."

Seth brought his mount up close to Williams and coaxed it to lie down. Bennett assisted Williams in sliding his right leg over the saddle to the stirrup. On Seth's command, the highly trained horse rose up with

Jace comfortably in the saddle. Lydia held a slight grin of pride on her face as she thought of her training of Chester.

The procession moved out toward the Red River. Bennett led the group with the two mounted wounded rustlers in tow. Seth was second in line with Williams in tow, tied securely in the saddle.

Lydia brought up the rear leading a line of horses roped together. Deceased Deputy Grant and dead outlaws secured across the saddles.

Two and a half days later, a somber procession of Deputy Marshals crossed the Red River and entered Paris, Texas. Curious citizens stopped their activities to watch the sweat stained cavalcade pass through the town square on the way to the undertaker, the hospital, and the jail.

Word quickly spread throughout the town, "Marshals have been into the Indian Territory again and served swift and deadly justice to outlaws."

Reporters for *The Paris News*, and other news correspondents flocked to the U.S. Marshal's Office to inquire about the latest jaunt into The Nations. More specifically, they were highly interested in what role did the new Lady Marshal play in subduing the outlaw gang.

Speculation on the street ranged from "The Lady led the Marshals in a charge against a large gang of owl hoots," to "How many outlaws did the Lady Marshal shoot?"

At the U.S. Marshal's office, Marshal Franklin addressed a small group of reporters and correspondents.

"A few days ago, I sent five Deputy Marshals into the Nations to locate and arrest a gang of five horse rustlers. Now, they are back in town. That is all I can tell you at this time. After, and I do mean, *after*, the Marshals submit their report to me, my office will issue a statement that each of you will receive a copy of. Then, gentlemen you will have your information. Until that time, I expect to not read a word of this expedition in any published form. Good day to you." Franklin turned and entered his private office.

The news people looked at one another and shrugged. The Marshal's word was his bond and they would eventually get their story.

CHAPTER FIFTEEN

AN INTERESTING TESTIMONY

That evening, Lydia completed her official report to Marshal Franklin on the latest venture into the Choctaw Nation. She laid the handwritten report down on the small desk in her room and then closed her eyes for several long minutes as she reflected on her presence in Paris, Texas.

Someone once said that life experiences can flash through your mind within minutes or even seconds. This quiet moment was no exception for Lydia.

Paris was the only home she knew and now both her parents lay side by side in the cemetery. While studying in Dallas at the Academy, her father made a routine trip into the Indian Territory to show the wares and take orders for the company that had employed him for twenty years.

On this trip, he was caught without shelter in a freak thunderstorm. Drenched to the bone, Forsyth came down with a hard cough and cold. Upon arriving home in Paris, he made a visit to his old friend, Doctor Reynolds. His lungs filled and with fever, Forsyth was ordered to bed by Dr. Reynolds, as he feared pneumonia had its grip on the traveling salesman.

Treatment was not timely enough for Jonathan to recover. His weakened state along with wracking pain in his lungs consumed him.

Lydia, called home from school in Dallas, arrived only the eve before his passing. She stayed at her father's bedside speaking softly to him, telling him how much she loved him, for being the best father and raising her strong to be her own strong woman.

Upon graduation from the Academy, Lydia sought to return to her birthplace to make her life there. As she prepared to leave Dallas, by chance she read an article in the *Dallas Daily Herald* announcing the advertisement for "Deputy U.S. Marshals needed for the recently established circuit court at Paris."

Lydia knew then what she wanted to do with her life. The Indian Territory needed Marshals to enforce justice and she had need to be one of them.

Lydia blinked her eyes for a moment, then bolted upright in her straight backed wooden chair at the desk. She shook her head to clear her thoughts and then picked up her report to Marshal Franklin to re-read what she had written. Satisfied that she had correctly explained the events pertaining to the case at hand, she carefully signed and dated the document. She would deliver it in the morning.

Lydia reported to the Marshal's Office with her report in hand promptly at eight o'clock. She elected to wear her maroon riding skirt with matching jacket and white blouse on this morning. Her Colt was strapped to her waist and the Silver Star was pinned to her lapel. She wore her hair up and as usual, her grey cowboy hat and boots.

Ross Bennett and Seth Grimes were already seated in Franklin's office. Rosemarie motioned for her to enter and join them right away.

Franklin motioned Lydia to the third chair in front of his desk as he accepted her report. He sat back in his large chair and carefully read each report of the events in the Territory, reading Lydia's last.

Finally, William Franklin nodded his approval and related, "Each of you has written an excellent description of the incident and subsequent arrests in this case. I can now issue an official statement to the news reporters that have been itching for more stories of Indian Territory justice for their readers."

He pondered his next thoughts, "For now, I would like you, Marshal Forsyth, to go upstairs to the court attorney and deliver these reports to him personally. Answer any questions that he may have about our latest foray into the Nations. Bennett, you and Grimes will come with me to look in on Jace Williams. I have yet to receive his report on this incident."

The four Marshals stood and proceeded to their assigned tasks. Lydia had not yet met prosecutor Lyle Elliott, but word had it that he was a tough man when it came to justice in the circuit court.

She took her time ascending the stairs to the second floor of the courthouse and then walked slowly down the hallway studying signs on the glass of the various legal offices. She found the one that she sought about half way down the hall and, taking a deep breath, entered the office of the prosecuting attorney.

A dark-haired attractive young matron sat behind a wooden desk. She looked quite the legal business woman in her dark skirt and white tailored blouse complimented with cameo broach fastened on a black grosgrain at the collar.

The immaculately dressed woman looked up at the new arrival and smiled. "You must be the new Lady Marshal. I am Sarah Brooks. How may I help you?"

Lydia smiled back, relating, "Yes, I'm Lydia Forsyth. Marshal Franklin asked me to deliver these reports directly to Mr. Elliott. Is he available?"

Sarah replied, "Yes, Mr. Elliott anxious awaits your reports. And, I might add, may have some pertinent questions to ask you. Please have a seat and I will announce your arrival."

Lydia took a seat along the wall with the reports in her hand while Sarah Brooks moved toward the inner office of Lyle Elliott. She opened the door quietly and entered, closing the door behind her. Sarah reappeared within minutes announcing, "Mr. Elliott will see you now." She held the door open for Lydia.

Lydia entered the private office of Lyle Elliott whom she found was the epitome of a court trial lawyer. He stood six foot tall with dark wavy hair and neatly trimmed mustache. His eyes were steel gray, and piercing, which cast him as an intimidating figure for those whom he questioned on the witness stand.

Lyle stood behind his desk, and as Lydia moved into his office, he stepped around to the front of his desk to greet her with a smile and gesture to sit with him. He quickly appraised this slender, dark-haired Lady Marshal.

"Marshal Forsyth. I have received several first-hand accounts of your prowess with firearms, and your horsemanship. I'm curious. How did you acquire your skills for this job as Marshal?"

Lydia smiled in return, took a deep breath and responded confidently, "My father bought my first revolver and taught me the basics of caring for it and shooting it. Between Father and the Paris sheriff at that time, I learned quite a lot. As for horsemanship, I learned by observing horse training methods from an Indian friend in the Territory. Later, at the Ladies Academy in Dallas, a group of us girls wanted to start a Ladies marksmanship club. Well, an old Texas Ranger, by the name of Roan Phillips, volunteered to sponsor our club. He trained us in the art of shooting rifles. His instruction was quite to the point. Several of us young ladies practiced relentlessly in the use of Winchester rifles."

Lyle appeared quite surprised at Lydia's answers. "That is quite a resume. I can fully understand now why you wear that Star of authority. I am very glad to make your acquaintance. Now, if I may have those reports to peruse for a few minutes, we will speak further."

Lydia handed the sharply dressed attorney the three reports. He began reading them without hesitation. Lydia gazed around the office to find several landscape oil paintings adorning the walls. They interested her, as they appeared to be of the land near Paris.

Within minutes, Elliott finished reviewing the reports and nodding his head, observed, "All three of these reports substantiate one other. May I presume you will testify according to your statement at a trial for the two men brought back for justice?"

Lydia replied without hesitation, "I certainly will."

"Well, then, Miss Forsyth, I will notify you and the other deputies when the trial will commence and if your testimony need be heard. Thank you for bringing these documents to me. Have a good day."

The duo stood and before parting, Lydia spoke, "Who is the artist of these landscapes on your walls?"

Lyle blushed slightly as he looked toward the art for a second and then responded, "I'm the artist in question. I find it quite relaxing to paint. I paint scenes that interest me. Are you a student of art as well, Miss Forsyth?"

Lydia shook her head to the negative, "I just like good art. You did well, Mr. Elliott."

Marshal Franklin along with Bennett and Grimes sat in straight backed wooden chairs alongside the hospital bed of Jace Williams listening to his verbal account of the Territory venture. Jace ended his rendition with, "Bill, I got to tell you true. That Forsyth woman is something else. I couldn't believe it! She rode right on up to me and laid that hoss of hers down. In the next instant she was slinging lead like a seasoned gunfighter. She saved my bacon that day. I've got a whole different view of this Lady Marshal since I first met her. I'm proud to know her."

William Franklin, as well as Bennett and Grimes grinned back at Jace. "I don't hire but the best Marshals, Jace. You should've known that."

Jace could only raise his hand like he was swearing in and nod his head. He continued with yet another observation, "The Doc tells me that I will be laid up with this cast on my leg for about five more weeks. I guess that I'll be doing office work on crutches until I'm mended."

Franklin nodded his agreement. "Roseanne can always use help in the office. In the meantime, Ross—you, Seth, and Lydia will serve only local writs and warrants until those jaspers are tried in court. Jace, you rest easy. When you can use the crutches, report to my office prepared for that mundane office work that you enjoy so much."

The three Marshals rose and waved farewell to Williams. Franklin chuckled to himself as they left the hospital and returned to the courthouse.

Two weeks later, Bennett, Grimes, and Lydia attended the trial of the two surviving rustlers as witnesses for the prosecution. Lyle Elliott sat at his respective court station along with the assistant prosecutor. Charges of horse theft, assaulting Federal Officers, resisting arrest, and the murder of Deputy Marshal Bob Grant were read aloud.

The two accused entered a plea of Not Guilty and the presiding judge instructed prosecutor Elliott to proceed with his case.

Deputy Marshal Bennett was first on the witness stand. After swearing in, Elliott asked the question, "Marshal Bennett, "why were you and four other Marshals in the Indian Territory three weeks previous?"

"U.S. Marshal Franklin directed the five of us to proceed with open warrants into the Territory. Our goal was to investigate the vicinity of an old abandoned ranch two days into the Nations by a map drawn by an informer. The informant related that five men were holding stolen animals from the States at this location with plans to sell said horses within the Territory."

"And, Marshal Bennett, did you personally meet this so-called informant?"

"No, Sir. I did not. The informant is known only to Marshal Franklin."

Elliott thought for a moment before inquiring, "Do you see any members of that alleged horse theft group in this courtroom?"

"Yes, I do. They are seated beside Mr. Evans, their attorney."

"Thank you, Marshal Bennett. I have no further questions at this time. Your Honor, I hereby present signed statements by three of the Marshals involved in the arrest of the defendants to be entered in evidence."

Later, in that day, the defense called Whit Garner, one of the defendants, to the stand. Grant Evans looked the defendant in the eye and asked, "What were you five men doing at that abandoned ranch yard?"

Garner replied, "We are just regular horse hunters. We found them animals wandering loose in the Nations and rounded them up. We were looking to record the brands and try to find the owners."

Evans prompted the defendant, "Tell the Court what happened next."

Garner continued, "We was looking over the brands when this here bunch of riders appeared with guns drawn and quickly spread out. They came a-charging us. We thought they was rustlers so we mounted and drew our guns to protect ourselfs. They was half way to us when they started shooting. We had to defend and fired back. They wounded two of us, and kilt two others, afore they finally showed that they was Marshals. We had no chance to tell our story."

"Who was your foreman?" asked Evans.

"Our foreman was Luke Winters."

Without warning, Garner suddenly stood up in the witness box and pointed his finger at Lydia, "That there Lady Marshal shot him dead."

Judge Hunter pounded his gavel. "Order in the Court! Sit down, Mr. Garner."

Evans turned to Kyle Elliott, "Your witness! I have no further questions at this time." He returned to his seat beside the other defendant.

Elliott turned to the defendant, "You say that Marshal Forsyth killed your foreman. Who is your big boss? I mean, who is Luke Winters' boss?"

Garner was surprised that the question came up. He stammered a bit before answering, "Winters' boss calls hisself *Gabe*. None of us never saw him nor do we know where he is. Luke Winters always met with *Gabe* in private. He never told us nothing, but what *Gabe* told us to do."

At the mention of *Gabe's* name, Lydia's eyes widened in disbelief. The third man of the Schuler murder was alive and somewhere in the Territory. He was still operating with lawless abandon and apparently successful at it. She pondered that thought intensely as the trial ran its course.

In the end, the jury found the defendants guilty as charged, and sentenced to justice by hanging.

CHAPTER SIXTEEN

AN OLD FRIEND

The following week, Lydia along with Seth Grimes and a new cohort, Deputy Marshal Luke Canton, were summoned to the office of United States Marshal William Franklin.

Franklin explained, "I have received a request from the court to send a party of Marshals to the Talihina Jail in the Indian Territory to escort five men to the federal jail at Muskogee. You three are assigned to this duty. You will leave on the Frisco Railroad to Talihina at ten in the morning. You'll pick up the subjects in question and transport them by spring wagon to Muskogee. It should be about two days from Talahina to Muskogee. The Frisco line has reservations for you and your mounts. As usual, you will all carry open warrants should you encounter anyone who violates the law on your trip. Good journey to all of you."

The three Marshals departed Franklin's office. Once out in the corridor of the courthouse, Seth turned to his partners for this next venture and related, "I'm going to spend the remainder of the day with my family. We'll meet at the railroad station at about nine in the morning." He left for home.

Luke Canton nodded and smiled, adding, "I'm going to spend time with my fiancé. Grace and I plan to marry in two months." He and Lydia walked to the front entrance of the courthouse where he took his leave.

Lydia stood on the front steps pondering her next move. Before she had a plan in mind, Ross Bennett appeared behind her with writs in hand to be delivered before sundown. When he saw Lydia, his face lit up. "Good morning, Lydia. How goes it?"

Lydia grinned, "Well, Seth, Luke Canton, and I will be traveling to Talihina in the morning to escort prisoners to Muskogee. With a bit of free time, I'm going to take Chester for a ride. He loves a good run and I love to feel the wind in my face."

Bennett grinned, then hesitated a moment before replying, "Well, it shouldn't take me long to serve these three writs. Maybe we could have dinner together at the Town Square Café say, around seven this evening?"

Lydia brightened up as she replied, "Ross, I'd like that a lot."

Ross smiled at her, "Thank you, Lydia. I'll call for you at the hotel."

The two Marshals then went about their own business with Lydia looking for Frank Sutton and his horse taxi to take her to the livery to pick up Chester.

After saddling up Chester, Lydia led him out of the livery and mounted. She touched his flanks ever so lightly with her spurs. The anxious bay stepped out in a brisk trot. He was ready for the high-spirited run that he knew was coming. Lydia held a liking for a good run and always put it into her daily exercise routine for Chester.

Once through the town square, Lydia turned Chester south. When the pair met the open prairie, the horse moved into a steady gallop. Soon, Lydia shouted "Chester! Go!" and the gelding immediately jumped into a ground-eating run. After several hundred yards, she reined him in and then, slid out of the saddle to throw her arms around the animal and hug his neck. On such occasions it was obvious that the two of them were made for each other—born to the wind.

The mistress spoke softly to the horse as she stroked his neck and face, "Chester, tomorrow we will take a train ride for a few hours. You will be in a stock car with other animals and should fare well. I'll take you on board the rail car and bring you back off when we reach Talihina. I believe that this will be your first train ride. You'll be fine."

Momentarily, Lydia once again mounted and led Chester through his exercise paces concluding in an all out mile run of varying curves and circles until she spurred him to the edge of town and reined him into a dignified trot. Once back at the livery, she rubbed him down with potato sacks and laced his feed trough with grain as well as fresh hay. She spoke to her spirited partner the entire time and, before leaving, produced a delicious apple for his treat

Back at the Peterson Hotel, Lydia readied her travel gear for the next day including a check of her Winchester to insure it was in working order. She packed her duffle and then glanced at her timepiece, only to realize that she only had time to freshen up before meeting Ross Bennett for dinner.

The young woman poured water from the pitcher into the porcelain bowl on the washstand and chose a new bar of soap scented with what would become "her fragrance". As she washed her face, she thought of Ross Bennett.

As a handsome man with deep blue eyes, and light brown hair, Ross always held an easy smile for her and, from the very first of their acquaintance, treated her with respect. She pondered that as she readied herself for dinner. What was it about Ross that intrigued her?

At a quarter to seven, Lydia stepped out of her room attired in light beige blouse buttoned to the collar with dark brown riding skirt and matching waist jacket. Her Star was in one pocket and her Colt .41 Thunderer slipped down inside the other. She wore her hair to the collar without a hat.

She found Ross Bennett waiting in the hotel lobby. Lydia giggled a bit when he stood and gave her a gracious gentlemanly bow. The two of them laughed gaily as they slipped inside the eatery. Hostess Lynn Phillips quickly escorted the pair to a table for two in a quiet corner. Lynn thought they made a handsome couple.

For the next two hours, Lydia and Ross exchanged light conversation over a supper of roasted beef, potatoes and gravy along with sliced garden carrots and coffee. They delighted in a slice of apple pie topped with a slice of cheese.

Later, Ross asked to escort Lydia to the lobby of the Peterson hotel.

"I'd like that, Ross. Actually, I'd like to walk the town square before retiring. Are you game for a stroll?

Ross's eyes shined with pleasure at her request. "That's a wonderful idea, Lydia." He offered his arm and she took it. Together they made small talk as they strolled slowly around the square, looking at the wares in shop windows.

Near the end of their walk, Ross stopped her for a moment. He looked deeply into her eyes and said softly, "Lydia, I like you a lot. I'd like to continue to see you socially."

Lydia returned his gaze, "I like you also, Ross. Yes, we should continue to meet socially and perhaps, there might be a community social or dance in our future."

They bid each other a fond farewell in front of the Peterson Hotel lobby. They looked into each other's eyes and held hands for a long moment.

The following morning, Lydia, mounted on Chester, rode to the rail depot and found the stock assembly point. Seth and Luke arrived soon after. The three Marshals loaded their animals into the rail stock car before they walked to the rear passenger car to board the train for Talihina.

Lydia wore her regular trail outfit. The Silver Star was pinned on her shirt under a hip length jacket. The Colt revolver sat comfortably strapped to her slim waist and she wore calf-high boots with spurs.

The Pullman car passenger seats were wooden upholstered, double occupancy. There was one set of seats on either side of an aisle down the center of the car. A wood burning stove with tinderbox stood next to the front entrance to provide warmth during cold weather.

Lydia took a window seat at the rear of the coach while Seth made himself comfortable next to her. Luke took the window aisle across from them. The three Officers took note of the other passengers that boarded their car.

There were a couple of cowboys, an elderly woman accompanied by a younger brunette, a gentleman with his lady who appeared to be a livestock buyer, and a family of four bound for Fort Smith.

A quarter of an hour later, whistles blew. The giant wheels of the steam engine began to churn on the steel rails. The three companions braced themselves seconds before the train commenced a forward movement. The trip would take a few hours so passengers attempted to situate themselves as comfortably as they could. Several passengers held box lunches that they had bought at the depot.

Seth spoke quietly to Lydia, "Well, partner. It's about eighty-five miles direct to Talihina. This train should travel over fifty miles in an hour. I'm guessing it is close to a two hours ride. Think I'll take a brief nap." Seth crossed his arms over his chest and leaned back. He closed his eyes and then pulled his hat down over his face.

Lydia on the other hand was fascinated with the landscape and watched how it changed from mile to mile. There were periods of thick brush and stands of trees before a clearing emerged without warning only to become forest again. They passed through hills with thick grasses growing on either side of the tracks.

Soon, the terrain became familiar to Lydia. She recalled the area around the Choctaw Council encampment. This land was similar.

Luke likewise spent his time observing the landscape. He had limited experience in the Territory and thus used this opportunity to familiarize himself with the terrain.

Seth was correct in his assumption on the time. Near the two hour mark, the train slowed down with bell clanging and whistle blowing. Lydia peered in the distance to see several scattered wooden buildings on the horizon.

The conductor walked through the passenger car announcing, "Talihina! Fifteen minute stop to take on water and mail."

The train came to a loud wheel-spinning screeching stop. Passengers remained in their seats except for the three Marshals who departed from the rear door. They walked to the stock car where railroad handlers opened the sliding door and placed the unloading ramp to the ground.

Lydia, Seth, and Luke went aboard and guided their mounts off the train to the edge of a corral. They found a water trough and allowed their animals to drink.

Lydia took a moment to survey the town from their limited vantage point. She found it sparsely sprinkled with houses. A general store with post office, feed lot, one saloon, a livery corral, and the Talihina Jail stood on the main street. There were very few people on the dusty, dirt street.

Seth turned to her and remarked, "They's only some two hundred people, if that, who live here in Talihina. Most folks who live here support the farms round about the town."

Lydia replied as she looked around, "That appears about right, Seth."

On schedule, the engineer once again blew the whistle and rang the bell. He eased forward on the gearshift allowing the train to chug off into the distance toward Fort Smith.

The three Marshals mounted their respective horses and rode to the jail where they dismounted and looped the reins around the hitching post before entering the stone structure with barred windows.

Once inside, they met with the sheriff and two deputies. One deputy looked familiar to Lydia. She studied his features for a few minutes while Seth talked with the sheriff. The familiar deputy took note of the female Marshal and held a puzzled look upon his face.

Lydia suddenly smiled. She knew this man. It was a long ago friend of hers from the Choctaw Council area whom she met while traveling with her father. He was the Choctaw boy who had befriended her and during their time together taught her about the Choctaw manner of training horses and a bit of the native language. She recalled that she was "Danny" during those times. She had dressed like a boy and acted the part.

She had no doubt that her friend, *Shanafila*, otherwise known as *Blue Hawk*, would remember her after she introduced herself once again. Lydia felt a bit of excitement at this meeting. She wondered how she would be perceived after he found that she was his friend *Danny*.

Minutes later, Seth introduced Lydia and Luke to Sheriff Tomas Hunt and his deputies. When her friend heard the name Forsyth, he was taken back a bit. He looked closer at Lydia and she smiled at him saying, "Halito, chim achukma?"

Blue Hawk was stunned. Lydia held out her hand to him, "I am Danny. My father, Jonathan Forsyth, dressed me as a young boy to visit your people when I traveled with him. It is well that he did."

Blue Hawk immediately recognized Lydia's voice. He quickly grasped her hand and with a smile replied, "It is good to see you again, my friend. We had many fine adventures together back then. Now, you are a Lady Marshal. I can respect that for you have traveled the land of the Choctaw and know some of our language. You know what to expect and can live off the land as I. This land remains dangerous; however, I see you have learned to wear the Silver Star. I am proud to call you my friend, Lydia."

Following the introductions, Seth inquired of Sheriff Hunt, "How soon will our five prisoners be ready to travel? We would like to get on the road to make good time before dusk."

Tom Hunt motioned to his deputies, "We can have the spring wagon with the five men and provisions for one day ready within an hour. Come with me to the cell block. I'll identify them for you. We have two for making whiskey illegally in the Nations, two for mail robbery, and one identified as a wanted murder suspect. When arrested, all surrendered peaceably."

Hunt turned and moved toward the entrance to the cells. Seth motioned for Lydia and Luke to follow. Once inside, Sheriff Hunt stepped to the first cell. Two men in their later years stood before them. Their gray beards and stooped shoulders bore witness to lives worn by hard living.

Hunt remarked, "Raise your hand when I state your name. This here is Marcus and Oliver. They used to moonshine over in Arkansas, but got run out by Judge Parker's Marshals. They've come up here in the Nations continuing to make their whiskey, and they were caught selling some."

He moved on to the next cell. "These men go by Vickers and Parker. They held up a stagecoach and pilfered mail. Well, we caught them with the goods."

Vickers stood tall and with gruff voice, "We found them pouches in the brush! We were trying to put all that mail back into the bag to turn in."

Parker remained seated on his cot, glaring at Sheriff Hunt. His eyes then focused on Lydia, "Well now, ain't you the purty looking one. You a schoolmarm or something? Yah! That's it. She's a schoolmarm and she is going to teach us a lesson."

Vickers interrupted, "Nah! She ain't no schoolmarm. She's packing iron."

At the third cell, Hunt indentified a man called "Jackson". He was a burly, dark mustachioed man some six foot two. This man remained reclined on his bunk. He glared at the law officers and audibly announced, "I'm innocent! I didn't kill nobody! That warrant was issued by a lily livered judge bought and paid for by the SOB that stole my ranch and killed my partner."

Seth spoke up, "I seem to remember that warrant. Innocent or not, you need to answer that warrant so things can be sorted out. If what you say is true, Marshals will investigate your claim."

Lydia observed the man carefully. Although he seemed uncooperative, she felt that he might be telling the truth as she had heard of accounts of such activities.

After visually displaying the persons to be escorted to Muskogee, the officers returned to the outer office. Sheriff Hunt recommended, "It will be about an hour. That café across the way is small but they do serve good coffee and sandwiches, if you've a mind for some."

An hour later, Seth, Lydia, and Luke stood to horse as the five men shuffled to the spring wagon where deputies leg shackled them to the floor of the wagon. Another deputy brought out a duffle of camp supplies along with provisions of one day and placed it into the wagon at the driver's seat.

When all was ready to move, Deputy Blue Hawk climbed to the driver's seat. The young Choctaw grinned at Lydia and announced, "Well, you Marshals don't know the Territory like I do. I'll be your driver for the trip." And with that announcement, he settled back, took up the reins of the two horse team, and slapped the horses lightly into a walk towards the northwest.

Lydia and company fell in beside, and behind the wagon as it jostled and swayed along the dirt road lined with ruts of wagon wheels.

The prisoners reclined as comfortably as they could make themselves for the less than desirable journey. At the rate of roughly twenty-five miles a day by wagon, the party scarcely made fifteen miles out of Talihina before dusk. They would make up for that on the following day.

With the prisoners shackled together at the ankles around a thick tree that evening, a small fire was lit and coffee served up all around. A light meal of cold biscuits, warmed beans, and a stick of jerky made for a sparse supper.

Seth Grimes and Luke Canton sat away from the fire enjoying quiet conversation while casually observing the prisoners in their muffled banter.

Lydia and Blue Hawk sat near the campfire renewing their acquaintance. Blue Hawk pleasantly related, "I married a good friend of mine. Her name is Little Dove. She has born me a son of a year now. We have a small house at the edge of Talihina. Dove is a good woman who keeps our home clean and our garden plentiful. I could ask for nothing more. She weeps sometimes when I am out riding the Nation in search of lawbreakers."

He sat back, a bit more relaxed and then continued, "Enough about me. What of you, Lydia? What happened to your father, Jonathan? How did he die? What have you done since we last parted?"

Lydia fondly recalled her father as she paused before speaking, "Hawk, my father took sick and passed to the Spirit several years ago. He was in a heavy rainstorm and became very ill. I completed school and returned to Paris where I worked to become a Deputy United States Marshal. I have met someone, another Marshal. I believe that he is fond of me. Yes, I am growing to like him very much also."

Blue Hawk nodded and then softly spoke, "It is good that you have found someone you care for. I wish you good fortune in your life. Now, let us prepare for sleep, for tomorrow will be a very long day."

Within minutes, Seth announced, "Luke, you take the first watch. Hawk, you take the second, Lydia take the third watch and I will watch until sunup when we will break camp and proceed to Muskogee. I do caution all that the area around Muskogee is most wild and dangerous for any lawman. I heard it said that there were more lawmen killed within the fifty mile radius of Muskogee than anywhere else west of the Mississippi. Take that information to heart."

It was near two in the morning when Hawk lightly nudged Lydia's boots to awaken her. She sat up slowly and stretched a bit before standing and looking around the campsite. Hawk spoke softly, "Time for your watch, Lydia. I'll be over there next to the wagon."

Lydia nodded before taking her canteen for a drink of water. She poured a bit in her hands and splashed her face a bit. That awakened her. She reached for her Winchester and moved to a place between the prisoners and the wagon, a short distance away from the glow of the fire.

She slowly looked over the men in shackles and determined all were asleep except for one, Jackson. She moved toward him and asked, "Why are you not asleep like the others?"

He replied, "I was thinking, would a Lady Marshal really shoot me if I tried to escape?"

Without hesitation, Lydia replied, "In an instant! Like Marshal Grimes said, you must face the court to clear yourself. He is a man of his word. He said that he would make sure your case was thoroughly investigated. I believe him. Now, best that you try and get the next few hours of rest. We will be moving out soon enough."

Jackson seemed to take Lydia's words to heart and turned to go to sleep.

Travel the next day was without incident and toward late afternoon the escort party with prisoners in tow entered Muskogee. They rode directly to the Federal Jail. Lydia took in the city as they rode down the main street. There were saloons enough as well as more than one bawdy house. Gambling houses were common as well. Curious citizens watched the small cavalcade make their way to the jail.

Of particular interest was that the party included an attractive young woman wearing the Star of Deputy U.S. Marshal who rode beside the wagon of prisoners. Lydia became the instant subject of inquisitive chatter and pointing fingers as she rode down the main street.

Two young men clutching journals in their hands followed quickly to keep pace with the prisoner wagon. Lydia contemplated their purpose, while scanning the crowd. She was careful to keep Chester in check.

When the prisoner entourage reached the Federal Jail, Seth dismounted and went inside. Luke and Lydia remained mounted. Minutes later, he returned with three guards who took charge of the five men the Marshals had delivered. Once relieved of their prisoners, Seth announced that he had been handed a telegram from Marshal Franklin.

"Franklin wants us to ride over to McAlester to pick up two men from the Federal Jail there. We are to escort them back to Paris. In the meantime, we'll rest here for the night to get an early start in the morning."

Blue Hawk looked to Lydia. "I must be on my way back to Talihina now. It was very good to see you again, Lydia. Perhaps, we will see one other again soon. You take care." He then turned his spring wagon back down the road south and faded from view. Lydia was glad that Blue Hawk had a life that suited him.

Seth pointed out the hotel down the street, "One of the federal guards suggested that the three of us get rooms straight away. We'll take our supper at the restaurant next door to the hotel. The guard said that it has the best food in town. Let's lead out over to our lodging. I was also told that there's a stable out back of the establishment to care for our mounts."

Lydia and Luke dismounted and led toward the hotel. Lydia was momentarily approached by the two journalists she had observed earlier. They had waited patiently for an interview.

Rob Martin spoke up, "You are somewhat of a celebrity. We don't know of any other Lady Marshals who ride the Indian Territory. May we talk to you? Why did you become a Deputy Marshal? Our readers will be highly interested in your story."

Lydia stopped abruptly and turned to face the young men, keeping tight rein on Chester. She thought for a moment before responding, "Thank you for your interest. I aim to earn a reputation for being a dedicated officer of the law on the side of justice. Good day, gentlemen."

She turned, leaving the two newspapermen standing in the street, each with a bewildered expression on his face. Both men eventually turned to walk off. They scribbled notes about Lydia's appearance, as well as her statement about being a Deputy Marshal.

CHAPTER SEVENTEEN

RIDE TO MCALESTER

Lydia and her two partners Seth and Luke tied their mounts at the hitching rack in front of the Muskogee Hotel. They registered at the reception desk with a very talkative clerk.

George Landers greeted the trio with, "Welcome folks. Welcome to our enterprising community. Since the Federal Court was established here in Muskogee last year, the city has been really growing.

Will you be staying long?"

The law trio shook their heads.

"No? Well, I hope you will have a pleasant visit while you are here. Please sign my register with your name and where you are from."

After registering, Seth inquired about a stable for their mounts. They were directed to a small stable for horses of guests in the rear of the hotel. As they saw to their animals, Seth chuckled a bit. "That ole boy sure loves his town."

He continued by suggesting, "I think that a hot bath is in order before supper." Lydia was all for a good relaxing soak also. She hoped that the hotel had more than one tub.

Promptly at six o'clock, the trio met in the lobby and walked next door to the restaurant where they partook of the house specialty. Country fried chicken, mashed potatoes with gravy, and garden fresh green beans were the order of the day. Freshly baked rolls and hot coffee complimented their meal. Afterwards, they indulged in warm apple pie and a second cup of Arbuckle's.

Speaking over dinner, Seth mentioned, "It seems to me that it is nigh about sixty some odd miles to McAlester. Our horses are in good shape. I figure we can make it by dusk tomorrow."

At daybreak, the three Deputy Marshals were in the saddle once again and on the road. Lydia reminisced about when she met Mr. and Mrs. McAlester. It was on a sales trip into the Territory with her father, Jonathan. She smiled, remembering their hospitality.

Seth rode beside Lydia, allowing conversation. They rode for about an hour, dismounted and led for thirty minutes and then, remounted to ride for another hour before dismounting and leading again.

Lydia spoke to Seth, "This is a smart way to save our animals' endurance. Where did you learn it?"

Seth grinned as he replied, "To tell the truth, I spent a few years in the Army, the cavalry to be exact. Well, we learned real quick that your horse is your best friend when out in the wilds. You must take care of him and he will take care of you. Anyway, this is the old cavalry method of traveling long distance, all the while keeping your mount trail worthy."

Lydia considered the veteran lawman's words, then replied, "Now I understand my father's manner of driving our wagon on his trips through the Territory. We rested our animals in a similar fashion. Thank you, Seth. I've learned a lot from you since we've been partnered up."

"You are a keen learner, Lydia. I like that in a young Marshal. In fact, case you didn't know it yet, several of us old-timers are of the same thought."

Lydia blushed. Without warning, Chester slowed his pace and his ears pricked up. Lydia noticed it immediately and raised her guard. She signaled to be on alert.

Lydia spoke in almost a whisper, "Seth! Luke! Something's amiss. Stop to listen!"

The three Marshals reined in their mounts and listened carefully. There was no sound. There were no birds chirping. Not a breath of wind could be felt. Then, a slight wind caressed Lydia's cheeks, but she paid it no mind as her eyes scanned the terrain to the fore of them. She thought, "Father always said that the absence of nature's sounds signifies danger."

The trio's eyes darted forward and sideways. Luke slowly turned in the saddle to view their back trail.

A split second later, a rifle shot split the air and Luke jerked back in the saddle clutching his right shoulder. He waivered and then fell to the ground, the breath knocked out of him. Seth immediately dismounted and moved to Luke's aid.

Lydia's eyes flashed ahead to the left and with a deep breath, she sunk left spur to Chester's flank. In a flash, the bay jumped into a dash toward the heavy brush on the left. She coaxed him through the tangles for a few minutes, then turned back toward the road, bearing more to their left side.

Once again, rifle fire rang out. It was returned by revolver fire from the front. Seth had dragged Luke to the far side of the road into a gully before searching out the culprit.

Lydia rode to within thirty yards of the road and dismounted. She left Chester standing with reins trailing while she drew her Winchester before creeping forward. At ten yards, she spotted movement in the heavy grass. The rifle fired again. This time, she located the source. The young Deputy moved stealthily forward.

Lying in the grass ahead of her was the figure of a big man. He held a rifle and seemed to be carefully selecting his target for the next shot.

When Lydia levered a round into the chamber, the ambusher heard the sliding mechanism. He turned abruptly to stare at a woman sighting a Winchester directly on him.

Lydia yelled out, "Federal Officer! Drop that rifle and throw your hands up!"

The burly bearded man rose from the ground with rifle in hand screaming, "The Hell I will!"

Lydia's reply was, "You're dead if you don't."

The man threw his weapon to shoulder and Lydia fired her first round directly into his chest. The man staggered backward, still trying to draw a bead on her. Her second bullet went through his middle. He fell straight back and lay on the ground, his body jerking with involuntary motion.

Lydia moved forward to stand over the stranger. She asked quickly, "Why did you shoot at us?"

The man's eyes went wide as he coughed blood and sighed, "Told to kill three Marshals before they got to McAlester. Gabe told me."

The man coughed more before taking his last breath. Once again, Lydia heard mention of that familiar evil name. She mouthed the words that seared through her mind, "This man, *Gabe*, seems to have henchmen everywhere. What is his motive to kill us before we get to McAlester? Does it have anything to do with the men we are supposed to escort to Paris? I wonder!"

Lydia left the ambusher where he lay in death and called Chester to her. The bay eagerly trotted up allowing her to remount. "Come on, Chester, on to the road and see how Luke and Seth are doing."

She touched spur to his flanks and he trotted through the thick grasses and up onto the road.

Seth and Luke were some thirty yards away in the gully.

Seth waved to Lydia, "Go find our horses! They went that a-way!" He pointed in the direction in which they had come. Lydia turned Chester down the road and found both animals grazing less than a quarter mile away. She rounded both up and drove them back to the men.

Seth removed Luke's clean spare shirt from his saddlebags, and with belt knife, cut the sleeves off to make a compress and bandage strips with which to tie them in place. The compresses were snugly tied in place, and the bleeding stopped. Luke determined that he could still ride with his arm in a sling.

Seth removed Luke's bandana and folded it into a triangle. Once it was placed around Luke's arm, he adjusted it for comfort. The bullet was still lodged in Luke's shoulder. He would have to make it to McAlester for medical treatment.

Standing to horse, Luke took several deep breaths and then nodded to Seth and Lydia to help him into the saddle. Once situated, he took another deep breath and exhaled. "Damn! Just a few inches more to the left and I wouldn't be riding on like this. I am O.K. There must be less than forty or so miles to McAlester."

On the road again at last, the three Marshals rode side by side. Lydia told her companions about the man they left behind. "I got him. He chose not to surrender. He commented before he died that *Gabe* told him to kill all three of us before we got to McAlester. Is there something about the men we are supposed to escort that we don't know?"

Both men were silent for some time before Seth replied, "I am more concerned about how this *Gabe* knew that we three were coming for those men. It seems to me that there is an informant in place at Muskogee. We got to find that person and see justice there."

Lydia remarked, "I hadn't thought about that, Seth. You're absolutely right. Someone had to have passed information. Who all knew about that telegram from Franklin?"

Again, Seth rode in silence as he thought about her question. Finally, he related, "Well, there was the telegraph operator, the Deputy Marshal who passed the telegram to me," and as he thought further, he said, "and the jailer who was present when the Marshal spoke to me about the contents of the telegram."

Seth went silent again, as if he was calculating something of importance.

Lydia had his response on her mind. She thought, "We stayed overnight. Anyone of the three had enough time to contact the shooter and have him waiting for us on the road to McAlester. Who most would want to gun down three Deputy Marshals? And why?"

The three partners rode on through the day to arrive in McAlester at twilight. They went directly to the doctor's office for medical assistance for Luke. While Luke was being attended, Lydia and Seth went to the McAlester Federal Jail to inquire of Chance Weston, the Chief Deputy, about who they were to take on to Paris.

Chance Weston gave the pair a questioning stare. "I don't know what you are talking about! I don't have anyone in this jail bound for Paris. I've received no authority to release any of these prisoners for transport there."

Lydia and Seth looked at one another. Lydia spoke first, "We've been set up for a killing, Seth."

Seth nodded and then asked a critical question of Weston, "Did you get any recent prisoners from within the Territory here?"

Weston immediately answered, "Well, yes. Matter of fact, Deputy Marshal Grant Williams brought two men in from the Choctaw Nation that he arrested three days ago. They are both warranted for murder. Why do you ask?"

Lydia responded, "Where is Marshal Williams?"

Weston answered, "Unfortunately, Williams stayed overnight and when he went to the livery for his horse the next morning, someone shotgunned him in the livery. The Sheriff is investigating his murder at this moment."

Seth spoke quickly, "I want both of those men readied for escort to Paris by tomorrow morning. And, I don't want anyone else to know that. We will take them on the train to Sherman and then on to Paris. Trust me, Williams, you don't want those men in this jail."

Williams was dumbfounded but nodded his agreement.

Lydia and Seth left the Federal Jail and walked back to the doctor's office for Luke. As they passed an alley, a slovenly figure appeared from behind a trash bin, shotgun in hand. He raised it toward the law duo.

As one, Seth and Lydia reached for their revolvers. Lydia drew, cocked, and shot the intruder without hesitation. Seth surprised her by drawing his Colt. Holding it in front of him, he palmed the hammer in a fanning motion. Three bullets hit directly into the man's chest. The man slammed to earth with four rounds in his body.

Sheriff's men arrived quickly and took charge of the dead ambusher, as well as taking statements from the two Marshals. The man's body was placed in a cart. Seth and Lydia stood in silence collecting themselves.

Lydia turned to look at Seth. "Just how did you do that, Seth? I want you to teach me how to do that."

Seth looked at Lydia and nodded. He opened the cylinder of his Colt and emptied it. Then, he held the weapon in front of himself. He turned slightly from side to side and Lydia took in his every move. Seth then palmed the hammer of his Colt back while he pulled the trigger. He repeated this movement again and again until he had completed it six times.

He related, "Hold your Colt aimed at your target, cock the hammer with the palm of your hand and pull the trigger but don't release it. Keep palming the hammer for as many rounds as you want to shoot. It's called *Fanning the Revolver*."

Lydia nodded her understanding and vowed to practice it daily until she was proficient in the method.

Next, Seth posed a thought to Lydia, "Let's go visit that rail station.

I have some thoughts about how we will take these men on the train tomorrow."

They turned on their heels and headed for the rail station where Seth asked his critical question of the stationmaster. "Will the train to Sherman tomorrow have an Express Car?"

The man's answer was affirmative, and Seth asked his next question, "And, is there a secure cage in that Express Car."

Again, somewhat puzzled, the Stationmaster replied, "Yes, there is a security cage in the Express Car?"

Seth broke out in a big grin. He motioned to Lydia to follow him outside. There, he turned and said, "Well now, that is mighty interesting. We are not taking those two men to Sherman in the traditional way. We aren't going back in the passenger cars, we are going to put them guys in the Security Cage and we will all be in that car with them."

Lydia also grinned with that idea. Anyone knowing of the escort would think that the men would be in the passenger cars.

The next morning, three Deputy Marshals took charge of two men from the McAlester Federal Jail. Both appeared to be hard men. Both were tall, lanky, weathered, and bearded. One had a deep scar below his left eye that ran down the outside of his cheek. The second walked with a limp. The prisoners glared with disgust as they looked over the trio tasked to transport them to Paris. The two naturally wondered about the female Marshal. Lydia moved with ease around the criminals. And, she looked as though she could handle that Colt strapped to her waist with ease, too.

Thirty minutes later, both prisoners were shackled wrist and ankles inside the Express Car of the train to Sherman. Lydia observed that the eyes of both men darted around at their predicament. Their expressions changed from ones of arrogance to ones of doubt. She further noticed that they began to sweat, although it was not unusually warm inside the car. Lydia keenly took it as a sign that they were worried.

The prisoners bound for trial quickly realized that they were surrounded by three Deputy Marshals, and three Wells Fargo Express Agents all armed with shotguns. They were extremely uneasy. The train arrived in Sherman, Texas on schedule and without incident.

Seth commented to Lydia and Luke, "Now, the most dangerous part begins. From here on out, we three are the only law until we get those sixty-some miles to Paris behind us. A lot can happen between here and there."

C H A P T E R   E I G H T E E N

A DANGEROUS ROAD TO PARIS

Upon arrival in Sherman, Texas, the train ground to a jolting stop. When the Express Car doors opened, a Wells Fargo wagon and three Wells Fargo guards were waiting as per company protocol.

Seth had the Express Agent unlock the security cage allowing him to retrieve the prisoners.

"Now then," he said, "you two will get to your feet and come peaceably." He took them to the door where the Express guards assisted them into the wagon and sat them down.

Seth addressed the guards, "We'll take these hombres to the Sherman Jail. I would appreciate your help to watch them while my partners and I pick up our mounts and obtain supplies for our trip to Paris."

The guards gladly accepted the chance to assist Deputy U.S. Marshals.

Meanwhile, Lydia and Luke had gone to the livestock car toward the rear of the train to offload their three horses. Lydia stroked Chester's face and neck, "How was the train ride? Well, we are going to take a long ride very soon. I just know that you'll love that."

When the three Marshals had mounted, the Express driver clucked to his team and the group moved to the jail. The Express guards were accustomed to hauling shackled men, and kept close eye on them. Seth expressed his gratitude for their service, "Thank you, men, we appreciate your help with our charges."

Job done, the Express wagon moved off toward their office. The three Federal Officers took the two men inside the jail. Seth requested that Sheriff Whitley hold them until he could secure a wagon for hire to transport the prisoners to the Paris Federal Jail.

The elder lawman locked the two men in a holding cell for safekeeping. Seth pointed, "This here is Jack Runnels. That is Albert Sontag. They are criminals with no remorse. Watch them carefully."

Seth turned to Luke, "Luke, you stay here to assist the sheriff. Lydia, go for supplies while I locate a suitable wagon. We should make it about half way to Paris by sundown. We'll camp overnight on the trail. We should make Paris about noon tomorrow."

Lydia walked over to Walton's General Mercantile to obtain overnight camping necessities. Seth moved quickly to the livery rental to secure a team and wagon that could transport their charges.

Lydia browsed the store before she selected a small campfire coffee pot along with a set of six tin cups. Next, she moved to a line of barrels and selected dried apples, and a fist full of beef jerky, along a dozen biscuits. At the counter, she had the clerk grind up enough Arbuckle coffee beans for two pots of coffee. That would have to do for the trail.

Lydia then moved to a counter in the rear of the store where a young woman took her order for three ham and cheese sandwiches wrapped in butcher paper.

After she paid for the goods, she stepped out to the boardwalk just in time to observe Seth approaching with the wagon and team of two horses.

Seth pulled up beside her and waited until she put the sack of supplies into the bed of the wagon and climbed up on the seat beside him. "Didn't get much, Seth, but didn't think we should count on a social picnic this trip." She laughed as Seth chuckled loudly and nodded his head.

Five minutes later, the pair pulled up in front of the jail. They dismounted to enter the jail with the three sandwiches. Fortunately, the prisoners had been served a lunch.

Luke had a cup or so of hot coffee or so brewed by the sheriff. He was thankful for the thick sandwich that Lydia handed him. The law trio sat in a corner in the jail office near a wood stove to eat their lunch.

Right after noon, with their charges loaded in the wagon bed and chained to the floor, the entourage proceeded down the Sherman Road toward Paris.

Luke drove the wagon with his horse trailing behind. Lydia rode the point position while Seth brought up the rear, "So's I can keep watch on these bad hombres."

Lydia kept a steady pace practicing the travel method that Seth taught her. Her eyes continually scanned the terrain ahead and to the sides of the road. She sharpened her senses by carefully listening to nature. Nothing seemed out of the ordinary.

Toward sundown, Lydia spotted for a campsite just off the road. She found one to their right side next to a creek that followed the road. She motioned for Luke to follow her off the road where brush offered protection.

They made camp. The prisoners were chained to a tree. Seth built a small fire while Luke watered the horses at the creek. Lydia got fresh water from the creek and made a pot of coffee. When the strong brew was ready, she passed out a large piece of jerky and a few dried apples to each, along with a tin of coffee. Lydia took note of the evening sounds as she listened to gentle splashes on the water along with the occasional croak of a frog.

The prisoners, Runnels and Sontag, eyed the Marshals intensely as they ate their meager supper. Both followed Lydia's every move with lust in their eyes. They held a secret between them—a deadly secret. The two men were certain that they would never reach that jail in Paris. They held favor with *Gabe*. That man would not let them down. He would arrange for them to go free somewhere along this road from Sherman to Paris. They pleasured themselves with evil thoughts about what lie in store for this female Marshal once they were shunt of their manacles. It was only a matter of time.

Seth turned to his partners in a whisper, "Luke, you take the first watch. Lydia will take the second. I'll take the final watch until we saddle up and move onward. Be extremely careful on your watch. Do not let those shackles fool you; these men are extremely dangerous."

Lydia's watch began without incident. She took up her rifle, checked the loads and action before settling just outside the glow of the campfire.

She sat with her back against a tree and listened carefully to the sounds of the night.

In the darkness, came the hoot of an owl that set the stage for a great winged bird to launch from a tree nearby tree a few moments later. The large bird flew through the camp before swooping upward into the dark night air.

Lydia was reminded of an old Indian legend she had heard as a child. The folklore related that, "*To hear the hoot of an owl and then to see it in flight was an omen of death.*" She shuddered at the thought for a moment, before returning to reality. The horses were calm. The four men in the camp slept.

Lydia occupied the remainder of her watch listening to night sounds that should be there—the opera of frogs, the symphony of crickets, the gentle splashing of fish feeding in the creek. Near four in the morning, she awakened Seth for his watch before moving to her blankets. Her Colt remained close to hand as taught to her by Jonathan.

Lydia was awake before dawn to make another pot of coffee. She distributed the remaining biscuits with dried apple along with a tin cup of coffee to each man. Seth and Luke ate quickly and then loaded the two captives into the wagon. The two men were then shackled securely to the wagon bed.

Again, Lydia rode the point while Luke drove the wagon. Seth rode behind to keep a vigilant eye on what lay behind them.

Ten miles fell away as they pressed on to Paris. In a clearing, Lydia saw a line of freight wagons approaching from the east. She drew Chester up short, then motioned for her cavalcade to stop. She drew her Winchester and held it at the ready.

As they drew nearer, Lydia counted five wagons and recognized Fred Hammond, freight boss from Paris. She remembered two of the other drivers. Hammond, upon seeing Lydia, held up his hand in a greeting, and halted his freighters for a breather.

"Hello, Marshal Forsyth. Fancy meeting you out here on this lonely road. H-m-m-m, appears like you are bringing in some bad ones, huh?"

Lydia nodded as such.

Hammond addressed Lydia with a serious face. "Marshal, can we light down for a few minutes and mosey over to the side of the road?" He pointed to a few yards away.

The old freighter and Lydia dismounted and led their horses off the road a short distance. Lydia knew Hammond wanted a private conversation.

"Marshal Forsyth, I may be wrong, and I hope I am, but I believe you may have some trouble waiting you about four miles up the road. We sighted near a half dozen men settling down along either side the road. My first thought was that they were going to jump us, but we just passed on by."

Hammond waited a moment, letting Lydia ponder his words. He continued, "They sure weren't farmers. In fact, they looked loaded for bear. I wondered just what they might be waiting for. Now that I see you folks, I can imagine what they may have in store for you. You be careful."

"Thank you, Mr. Hammond for your concern. We will be very careful. You have a good trip to Sherman." Hammond and his freighters waved farewell to the Marshal party as they passed and continued on the road west.

Lydia shared her news quietly with Seth and Luke. She felt a giant knot tie up inside her. Nothing about what Hammond had said gave her any relief. She was, however, confident in her abilities, and those of her Luke and Seth.

Lydia turned to Seth, "Well, what do you propose that we do?"

Seth thought for a moment before replying. He grinned, "Old cavalry saying, *when outnumbered, surprise the enemy by charging right down on them and make every shot count.* I intend to shoot as many as them up ahead as we can as we charge right on through them. What do you think of that?"

Lydia nodded her agreement, "This is going to be revolver work. I'll take the left side of the road, you on the right side and we'll clear the way. Luke has his shotgun and his revolver for anyone who jumps up in front."

Seth laughed, "Lydia, you are a woman after my own heart. You knew exactly what I was thinking. Well, let's give them Hell!"

The entourage moved down the road with Lydia in the lead. She paid close attention to nature, all the while noting Chester's change of pace. At near the four mile mark, Chester's ears suddenly pricked up as he shied toward the left of the road.

Lydia surveyed the brush that lined the road ahead. A flash of color in the weeds caught her attention. Instantly, she yelled out, "Let's go!" Seth spurred his mount to the right of the road in a galloping charge toward the color he spotted amongst the bushes.

Lydia touched spur to Chester causing him to jump the gulley. The trained horse stretched into a run along the brush lined ditch. She drew her Colt, holding it at the ready.

A figure loomed up to the left of her. She shot the man in the chest before swinging the revolver around to fire at another man head on. A third would be assailant jumped up from the ditch only to run towards the tree line. Lydia fired a round after him. He winced in pain before grabbing his leg and fell down screaming.

Suddenly, the blur of a fourth figure jumped up directly before her. Chester trampled the unfortunate ambusher. Lydia heard bones cracking as the man went down under the bay, shrieking in pain.

Seth was also engaged in the fray. Three men on his side of the road met their deaths by his revolver. Luke kept the wagon moving forward. Further along the road, two men jumped out of thickets, attempting to grab the team's bridles and stop them.

Luke leveled his shotgun at the first one and blasted him. The second man succeeded in grabbing hold of the harness. Luke held the reins tightly and kept urging the team to gallop forward.

The outlaw was dragging along beside the team still attempting to stop them. Luke drew his pistol and shot the man in the upper back. The intruder fell under the horses and the wagon ran over his leg. He screamed bloody murder at the pain. Luke holstered his weapon and cracked his whip.

The wagon team kept a steady run down the road. The prisoners in the back of the wagon were jostled all over the bed of the wagon but their shackles held firm.

The two men screamed, "Stop the wagon!" and, "Damn! You are going to kill us too!"

Luke paid them no mind as he continued at a fast pace until Seth and Lydia rode up alongside. They motioned him to slow the wagon down. They were a good two miles beyond the ambush that had turned deadly.

Seth checked on the two prisoners. Numb from the ordeal, the pair lay rather motionless with terror etched on each face. They could not believe how three Marshals could have shot hell out of nine men attempting to free them.

By early afternoon the three Marshal partners arrived in Paris. They rode directly to the Federal Jail where they were greeted by jailers, who helped remove the two prisoners from the bed of the wagon.

The wagon itself was splintered and shot to full of holes. The team of horses had gotten lathered and then cooled down without proper care. They needed the attention of a hostler.

Seth advised the jailers, "These men are Runnels and Sontag. They were arrested on felony warrants in the Territory and will be presented to the Circuit Court here. Lock them up separately as they are both criminals with dangerous friends who will stop at nothing to spring them."

Deputy Simon replied, "I've seen the posters on these two. We are glad to finally have them here in chains." The two jailers escorted the men to the cell block.

Seth turned to Lydia and Luke saying, "Well now. I suppose we should report in to Franklin and advise him on our latest undertaking."

Chuckling, he concluded, "And, he will be just *dee-lighted* that we are home safe and sound."

His companions caught the humor in Seth's comments. Their laughter released some of the tension of the past few days.

For the first time among his partners, Luke injected his own brand of humor—sarcasm. "Oh, yes! I am sure he laid awake nights worrying about us." With that statement, Luke became a full-fledged Deputy U.S. Marshal.

Lydia and Seth looked at one another with surprise. Seth grinned and drawled, "Seems like you are fast becoming one of us, Luke. Yes, you are one of us now."

The three turned their mounts toward the courthouse to report in to their boss man, United States Marshal William Franklin.

Animals secured to the hitching rack, the trio made their way to the steps of the courthouse to find Ross Bennett leaving the building. When he saw Lydia, a smile filled the young man's face, "Lydia! I am glad to see you back safely."

He didn't even notice her disheveled appearance after several days on assignment. The tossed hair, the dusty clothes didn't exist as far as he was concerned.

Lydia paused to greet her friend. "Ross, I'm glad to see you as well." The pair stood in silence enjoying the encounter.

Ross touched the young woman's shoulder, "There is a vaudeville show at the theater this evening. The presentation is a melodrama that is sure to be enjoyable. Would you like to accompany me to the theater this evening? It starts at seven thirty. We can have supper after the show."

Lydia smiled demurely, "Why, Ross. Now, how did you know that I love melodramas? I would love to spend this evening with you."

Ross Bennett smiled with, "The curtain is up at half past seven. May I call for you at your hotel by seven?

"I'll be ready Ross."

Lydia smiled then turned quickly to join her two partners at the top of the courthouse steps to report to Franklin.

The ordeal on the road earlier this morning had left her exhausted; however, the encounter with Ross and his invitation replaced exhaustion with exhilaration. She anticipated a hot bath, feminine attire and a date with one of the most eligible bachelors in Paris.

CHAPTER NINETEEN

CORBIN MORGAN

The following week, Lydia completed a round of serving writs to several local businesses before she reported back to Marshal Franklin's office for her next assignment. Ross Bennett and Seth Grimes were already out in the Choctaw Nation with federal warrants.

Lydia quickly learned that she was the only remaining Deputy Marshal available to cross over into the Territory on a special assignment.

William Franklin greeted Lydia with, "Marshal Forsyth, you have proven yourself capable of the rigors of your office. Your insight and remarkable knowledge of the Choctaw Nation landscape is commendable. I'm giving you the opportunity to prove yourself once again. Are you willing to be the only Officer on this venture?"

He paused to allow Lydia to gather her thoughts, "I want you to enter the Nations to perform a scout of the wilds in search of one Corbin Morgan, a bank robber. As usual, you will carry an open warrant in case you come across anyone violating a federal law. Morgan is rumored to roam the area between Garrett's Bluff and Talahina."

Franklin let the nature of the task sink in before he continued, "Morgan is a widower whose only son was in the care of a friend. This family lives on the north edge of Paris. I've been advised that his son Thomas, who is sixteen years old, recently left Paris for the Nations. We suspect that he searched for and joined his father."

Lydia acknowledged her assignment and returned immediately to her room at the Peterson Hotel to prepare for the journey. The young woman packed a duffle with toiletries, changes of clothing, and heavy socks.

Two hours later, she was at the livery saddling Chester for the ride. "Well, Chester, we are going back into the Nations again. This time, it's just you and me."

Chester was anxious for a long trail ride again and he seemed to understand that they would be traveling for a few days.

Trotting to the town square, Lydia stopped at the mercantile to replenish ammunition and gather travel food that she slipped into her saddlebags.

Not more than an hour later, Lydia crossed the shallows of the Red River into the Choctaw Nation.

Corbin Morgan led a band of misfits who stole their way through the Territory. Their primary targets were stagecoaches and mail wagons. In hard times, they would rob a general store or trading post off the beaten trails. When they robbed in Texas, the band would hightail it across the Red River into the Territory. "A man could lose himself in the wilds of the Indian Territory and never be found." Thus far, they had proven it true.

Once into the Choctaw Nation, Lydia sat Chester and pondered, "If I was running from the law, which way would I go?"

She knew that the most dense terrain ran northwest in the direction of McAlester. Riding that direction for a while seemed logical while scouting for tracks and recent travel. Her mind raced, "Perhaps, I might just come across the tracks of a young man who knows the manner of his father."

Lydia continued back and forth across the countryside until sundown. It was time to locate a good campsite for the night. With few minutes to spare, she spotted a stand of trees that provided shelter against the elements as well as an open view of the surroundings.

Chester was unsaddled, and left free to feed upon the tall grass. A stream beyond the trees gave invitation to indulge in a soaking at twilight, if only for a few minutes. Lydia disrobed, placed her Colt Revolver near the edge of the stream, and slipped into the cool water.

Moments later, Chester joined his mistress for a long drink to quench his thirst. Lydia playfully splashed water at him and the horse shook his head up and down to let her know he enjoyed it. Satisfied, he returned to his grazing.

The cool water proved refreshing to the young woman following the long ride through parched terrain. She dared not dally long for shadows were falling quickly. Lydia dressed quickly and then hurried to build a small fire to brew coffee and heat a tin of beans with bacon.

She took a tin cup filled with water, placing it on a stone next to the crackling flames. She took her sheath knife and carefully opened the can. She set it on a hot stone beside the fire. When the water in the tin cup boiled, she tossed in a small handful of ground Arbuckle's coffee. That would suffice for her supper this evening.

Following supper, Lydia moved out of the firelight to sit with her back against a tree. Her Colt and Winchester lay by her side. Momentarily, she closed her eyes and listened. There were the welcome sounds of nocturnal creatures, as well as Chester to keep her company.

When the small fire died down to smoldering coals, Lydia arranged the saddle as a pillow, opened her bed roll and placed one blanket to lay on and the other for cover. The weary traveler soon slipped off into a restful sleep.

Lydia rose at daybreak and refreshed herself in the stream with Chester in tow. After a cold biscuit and dried apple slices for breakfast, she saddled Chester, gathered up her bedroll and duffle. She rode out toward the east.

The morning ride brought two hours of crisscrossing rough landscape filled with heavy brush and multiple stands of trees. She avoided meadows and open spaces.

Without warning, she came upon a small campsite. The fire had been small and upon investigation, she noted an empty bean tin along with several saltwater taffy wrappers left behind. She smiled and thought, "This camper was likely a young person with a sweet tooth for taffys."

The young Marshal walked slowly around the site to study shoe prints in the dirt. Nearby were the hoof prints of a horse.

"I think that I've found Tom Morgan's first camp. Let's just see where these tracks lead."

Lydia tracked the camper's trail for several hours before she came upon additional tracks. There appeared to be three more horses joining the lone horse she followed.

The tracks led off together toward the southeast briefly before turning south. She sat Chester and wondered, "Could this really be Tom Morgan and did he actually meet up with his father and friends? I believe that they are headed back toward Texas."

Lydia's mind whirled, "There's only one way to find out. I'm going to follow this bunch until I know one way or the other."

Tom Morgan left his campsite shortly after sunrise that morning and traveled in an easterly direction. Two hours later, he was crossing a clearing when three familiar riders emerged from the tree line on his left. Tom was elated. It was his father, Corbin Morgan, in the company of Jock Taylor and Wesley Cobb.

Tom waved to the men and turned his mount toward them. He called out "Hello Pa!" as the men drew up to him.

Corbin Morgan gasped in disbelief. "Just what in the tarnation are you doing here in the Nations, Boy?"

Tom swallowed hard and stammered, "I—I thought you would be glad to see me, Pa! I don't like school. I quit. I want to ride with you and your friends. We could be a team, you and me."

Corbin scowled at his son, "This ain't no life for a boy. I promised your ma before she died that I would make sure you finished school and made something of yourself. You are going back to Paris straight away. We are going to take you to the Red and you will cross at Garrett's Ferry. From there, you will return to the Wilsons. You must apologize for making them fret over your absence."

"But, Pa! I want to be with you."

"There's no buts about it, Thomas Morgan! You are going back, else I'll whip your hide right here like the damn fool kid that you are."

Tom was devastated; however, he nodded his understanding. "All right, I'll go with you to Garrett's. But, I will be back when I'm out of school and a grown man."

Corbin replied curtly, "Follow me and don't lag behind. You never know who or what might be tracking us."

Morgan led out towards the south and Garrett's Bluff where Jesse ran the ferry across the Red River to and from Texas.

Two hours later, Corbin signaled his group to stop for a brief noon meal at a clearing.

Corbin and son Thomas along with their companions sat around a small campfire in the southern part of the Choctaw Nation. They had just finished their lunch.

The three men took out store bought cigarettes for a smoke. They passed a firebrand amongst themselves to light their tobaccos. They drew deeply on their pleasure and with a sigh, let the smoke slowly exhale. Ringlets of smoke floated on the light air current.

Tom took this moment to address his father again, "Pa, I'm sorry. I never meant to make you angry. I just wanted to be with you. Is there any way possible that we can be a family again, with a home of our own?"

Corbin swallowed hard. After a moment, he replied, "Son, I ain't angry with you. I'm more angry at myself. I didn't go to enough school to count it as going. Look at me now. I'm nothing but an outlaw—a wanted man. I cannot settle down in one place too long for fear that I will be caught and sent to prison. I want better for you, Son. Go back to school and do me proud."

Unbeknown to Corbin Morgan, his son, and the men resting in the camp, a lone figure crept stealthily through the brush and trees. The brush was thick and the figure had to sometimes circumvent and find another way to move forward.

Lydia Forsyth drew close to the edge of the noon camp. She stopped a moment to consider her surroundings. She observed every move these men made. Chester stood ground hitched some twenty yards behind her. The Lady Marshal virtually blended with the thick foliage around her.

Scanning the perimeter, Lydia found the four picketed horses. They were out of immediate reach of the group.

Lydia felt the fast beat of her heart. She took a deep breath, exhaled and stood straight. Winchester in hand, the young deputy moved directly towards the campsite.

Jock Taylor was the first to notice the movement, stunned for an instant before stammering, "We got—We got company!"

The campers immediately turned their heads toward the approaching figure. Corbin mouthed his surprise, "I'll be damned. It looks a lot like a woman with a rifle."

Lydia challenged, "U.S. Marshal! Drop your guns and grab sky!" Her statement caught all four men by surprise—for only a moment.

Jock Taylor snarled and yelled out, "Come and get mine! Ain't no woman Marshal going to take me in." His hand flashed for the Colt at his belt. It was the last thing he ever did. As his hand came up with the Colt, he cocked it, but not before a 44.40 Winchester slug smacked into his chest. A second round hit him close to the first.

Taylor grunted hard. He jerked backward with each hit, quickly slamming to the ground with glazed eyes staring into the sun. He died as violently as he lived.

Tom Morgan was in mid-draw when Corbin yelled, "For God's sake, drop that gun! I don't need you killed, too."

Corbin raised his right hand into air. He reached down with his left hand, unbuckled his gunbelt, and let it drop to the ground. He raised both hands high in surrender.

Young Tom Morgan stopped in mid-draw, releasing his grip on the Colt. It fell into the dirt. His eyes met his father's eyes. "I could have taken her!"

Corbin snarled at his young son, "You have no idea. That has to be Forsyth coming there and word has it that she is lethal. You do as I tell you, boy. You'll live a lot longer."

Tom scowled as he thought, "Huh! My old man seems deathly afraid of this *woman Marshal*. I ain't afraid of her. First chance I get, I'm going to wallop her good. Then, we'll see what goes here."

Lydia stepped cautiously forward. The Winchester never wavered as she looked at each man.

"Well now. Corbin Morgan, I have a warrant for your arrest. The charge is robbery and deadly assault. You boys shot up a few people when during your robberies."

Lydia looked toward the remaining two. "The young'un has got to be Tommy." Tom Morgan grimaced when he heard "Tommy." He thought, "Ain't no kid no more. I'm a man and I'm out to prove it."

When her eyes met the second man, he nodded. "Afternoon, Lydia."

"Good afternoon, Wes. That is you, Wesley Cobb? I do wish that you weren't with this bunch. Now, you <u>know</u> that I must take you in, too."

Wesley lowered his gaze, "I reckon so, Lydia. You got me fair and square."

Wes Cobb knew Lydia from way back. They were elementary school friends. Back then, Lydia was a slight wisp of a girl. Her long dark hair was usually worn it pigtails. She had freckles on her otherwise fair face. She had no freckles now. She was now an attractive woman and there was no mistaking the Silver Star of Authority pinned to her shirt pocket.

Lydia deftly produced two sets of handcuffs from her hip pocket before she had Corbin handcuff Wes Cobb. Then, she had Tom handcuff Corbin.

"Tommy, you'll have to wait until we get to my horse. Then, I have a set for you, too."

Tom Morgan scowled. Lydia's eyes left the young man briefly when she glanced at the fallen outlaw. Tom saw his chance to lunge at her.

The next thing the boy knew, he was lying on the ground in pain, holding on dearly to his crotch. Lydia had met his rush with her Winchester, swinging the butt straight between his legs. Tom had sunk to his knees, unable to speak.

Lydia allowed the smoke of confrontation to clear before she instructed the trio to secure the deceased Jock Taylor and his bedroll over his saddle. That task out of the way, her next order was for the group to mount and Corbin Morgan to lead the way toward Paris.

Corbin spoke to his son, "How do you feel now?"

"Like hell. She walloped me good. I never saw it coming."

"Serves you right," the father lamented. "I told you to back off. Still, think of it this a way. It may hurt, but it's a damn sight better than dead and slung over your horse like Jock."

Tom only grunted.

Lydia continued to keep her guard as they rode toward Texas. They would have to camp overnight and reach Paris by the following afternoon. She pondered their route as they rode. She wondered how close they could get to the Paris crossing before making camp.

Foremost in Lydia's mind was the nagging thought of just how she would remain awake and alert overnight. These men must be delivered to the Federal Jail tomorrow. Marshal Franklin's wisdom ran clear; there is always a need to have two officers take on warrants of more than one outlaw.

Near dusk, Corbin motioned toward a likely campsite. Lydia scanned the area and agreed that was a good place to halt for the night. Taylor's body was removed from his horse and laid out under a tree. The mounts were picketed a few yards off the camp edge.

Lydia watched carefully as Corbin and the others, still handcuffed, built a small fire with a ring of stones for safety. They pulled out their coffee pot to start a good brew. They also produced tins of pork and beans along with dried fruit and cheese.

Lydia's saddle bags held a similar version of supper. She enjoyed smoked ham, dried apples, and a small block of cheddar cheese. Wes Cobb offered her a tin of their coffee. It was quite strong, but just what she needed after the events of the day. It tasted good to her. She regretted that her classmate Wes Cobb, for his generosity, was indeed her prisoner.

Half way through their meal, their senses alerted. Riders were coming towards them. Lydia motioned for her charges to back away from the fire a bit. She cautioned, "Everyone mind your manners and you will be fine."

She drew her Colt for good measure. When in sight of the fire, the traditional hailing of a campsite rang out. Lydia was taken back when a familiar voice rang out, "Hallo the camp! May we enter?" She motioned

Corbin to answer the hail. In a loud voice, Corbin called out, "Enter and be welcome!"

In a moment, three riders entered the firelight circle. Lydia's heart skipped a beat when she recognized two of the men. It was Ross Bennett and Seth Grimes along with a prisoner of their own.

Lydia called out, "Ross! Seth! I am sure glad to see you!"

Ross was also surprised. "Lydia! What are you doing out here with—three prisoners?"

"It's a long story, Ross. I'll tell you after you get your mounts picketed and have some coffee with your supper."

Ross nodded and thought, "This ought to be a good story."

Seth and Ross situated their prisoner around the fire before moving to the picket line to unsaddle. The two Marshals approached the fire for a tin of coffee. They also had a meager supper of jerky and dried apples and chunks of cheddar.

After they had eaten, the prisoners bedded down for the night. Lydia and Ross sat a distance from the rest and she related her instructions from Franklin. She then explained about following Tom Morgan's trail and his meeting up with Corbin and friends. She told him of her decision to bring the gang members along with the teen back to Paris.

"To tell the truth, Ross, I anticipated finding the lad alone and persuading him to accompany me back to Paris. After finding the four of them, I thought it best to arrest all of them. I see now, that my decision to bring them all back together was not thought out sufficiently. I quickly realized that I might slip off to sleep and they would escape me, or worse. I am relieved that you and Seth found us."

Ross pondered her decision. "I suppose I would have handled it as you did. The difference is that Seth and I are more experienced with this sort of lawlessness than you are. Let this be a hard lesson, Lydia." He waited for her to acknowledge before grinning, "Just don't bite off more than you can chew."

Tears filled her eyes. The trauma of the day had finally caught up with her, "Oh, Ross! Thank you for your counsel. Yes, I will remember your advice."

The couple knew at this moment, they could not fully embrace one another. They touched hands for a brief moment. It would suffice. Together, they rejoined the others at the campfire.

Noon the following day found the cavalcade from the Nations across the Red River and into Paris, Texas. The first stop was the undertaker where they left the remains of Jock Taylor. When the party arrived at the Federal Jail, guards filtered out to greet them and take charge of their prisoners.

As a guard approached Tom Morgan, Lydia intervened. "Hold up there, Deputy. The kid doesn't go inside. He stays with me. He's not a criminal, only a run-a-way who now knows better."

The guard replied, "But, the young man is handcuffed."

Lydia responded, "I cuffed him just for a life lesson. Give his Pa a moment with him before taking him to the cell block. I'll look after them."

Father and son held surprised looks on their faces as Lydia removed the handcuffs from Tom's wrists. She deliberately stepped away from the pair to allow them a moment to say their goodbyes.

After hushed conversation with his son, Corbin turned to Lydia, "You are a good person, Marshal Forsyth. Thank you for your kindness."

He then faced his son, "Tom, now you know how it is with us. You go back to the Wilson family and ask their forgiveness. You stay in school and become a person that I can be very proud of. Perhaps after I get out of prison, we can get together to give me a chance to be a proper father to you, Son."

Father and son embraced each other. Each held mist in their eyes as the waiting guard took Corbin into the jail.

Tom turned to Lydia, "Thank you very much, Marshal Forsyth. I'll never forget your lessons. You don't have to come with me. I'm going back to the Wilsons and apply myself to the books."

Lydia nodded before she surprised Tom by giving him a hug. She whispered into his ear, "You are a good person also, Tom. Never forget that. Go now. Go to the people who care for you." Lydia and Tom shook hands. Tom mounted his horse and rode toward the Wilson residence.

Ross and Seth joined Lydia to ride to the Courthouse where they reported their most recent venture across the Red River to U.S. Marshal Franklin.

CHAPTER TWENTY

A PARTY OF MARSHALS

It was early September in Paris, Texas. Fall colors would arrive soon and along with it, a period of heavy rainfall. The Federal Court here had accumulated an abundance of warrants for numerous lawbreakers purportedly taking refuge within the Indian Territory.

The United States Marshal's Office was called upon to send a party of Federal Officers into the Choctaw Nation to round up those with warrants and transport them to the court for trial. Marshal Franklin assembled his available staff to form a posse for this tasking.

Standing before him were Ross Bennett, Seth Grimes, Lydia Forsyth, Jace Williams, and Nathan Starrett. He began the assignment with, "I have selected you five Officers because I have faith that you will prevail in your duty. I am instructing you to enter the Choctaw Territory and spread out to attempt to serve these ten warrants. Arrest the men you locate and bring them back to the Federal Jail here. I anticipate at least a week or more for this assignment. Take a pack animal with two weeks provisions for all. Undoubtedly, the weather may be cold and wet.

He hesitated briefly, "I implore you to use extreme caution. Several of these folks are warranted for vicious outrage and murder. Others have lesser charges. I trust that you will use good judgment in all undertakings. Are there any questions?"

Having no questions, Franklin dismissed his group of trusted Officers to prepare for their departure into the Territory.

Seth announced, "I'll take charge of the pack animal. I know of one that is readily available. I'll stop at the general store to purchase as well."

Bennett followed up with, "It's time to pack our duffle and ready our mounts for the long ride. We should be able to meet at the north of town within two hours. That will give us about six hours of good riding before dusk and our first campsite. I'll carry the warrants. We can review and distribute them tonight."

All of the five went their separate ways to prepare for the crossing. Lydia went to her room at the Peterson to make ready. She selected shirts, trousers, socks, and under garments for a two-week ride. After strapping the Colt around herself, she donned her favorite hip length jacket. Lydia took out her Colt .41 Thunderer, placing it as well as extra boxes of cartridges into her saddlebags.

Standing in front of the mirror, she took a final appraisal of her attire and decided that she was ready for two weeks in the field. Grabbing up her travel items, Lydia left the hotel to hail Frank Sutton's taxi to take her to Martin's Livery for Chester.

Chester was glad to see her and she talked softly to him as she saddled him and placed saddlebags, duffle, bedroll, and Winchester on him. Chester knew he was going on another trip and he was anxious to travel.

Lydia led the bay gelding out of the stables, mounted, and smartly trotted him to the designated meeting place. Bennett and Jace Williams had arrived before her. Their mounts were trail hitched and the two men were enjoying a leisurely smoke. Lydia rode up and dismounted, letting Chester's reins drop. He stood in place as trained.

Lydia took a seat on the ground with her partners and took out a peppermint to enjoy while they waited. Soon after, Nathan Starrett arrived and did likewise.

Nathan was a seasoned lawman. He had served several years with a Frontier Battalion of Texas Rangers through Indian uprisings as well as tracking border gangs. He was an expert tracker, having trailed many a bad man on the run. Now, he squatted comfortably and took out his makings.

Nathan did not pay for the new fangled store-bought packaged cigarettes. He still enjoyed rolling his own, as his Father taught him.

Some minutes later, Seth Grimes arrived with packhorse in tow. The packs seemed bulky to Lydia leaving her to wonder just what Seth had in mind when he shopped for vittles and such.

Seth eyed the group and drawled, "Well, I done my part. You folks just going to sit there or shall we commence this shindig?"

Moments later with all mounted, the party of Marshals rode to the Red River. They crossed the shallow waters into the Choctaw Nation. Once on the other side, they continued north towards the center of the Nation.

As dusk fell, the posse had ridden close to thirty miles into the Choctaw Nation. The Deputies were quite accustomed to the terrain, making it easy to locate a viable campsite for the night. They formed a picket line for their mounts and unsaddled them. The men formed a ring of large rocks and foraged for kindling and tinder to build their fire.

The evening air in September cools quickly. A blanket would be welcome with the low sixty-some temperature. Their fire would burn low all evening after supper was taken.

That evening the group enjoyed a surprise supper from Seth. He unveiled his poke of a delicious smoked half ham, a brick of cheese, a loaf of fresh bread, and most favorite of all, two tins of peaches.

After the filling meal, Bennett passed out two warrants to each Deputy. Lydia found that she had two warrants for distillers of illegal whiskey. She would ride westward in search of their still site. Jace drew two warrants for suspected horse thieves to the Northeast. Nathan's two warrants were for Army desertion and stolen government property. His search would take him southeast. Bennett and Seth Grimes took the remaining four warrants for suspected murder to the north. The group would ride their separate ways shortly after daybreak.

They next chose those that would perform the night's watch over the camp in four-hour turns. Nathan took the first watch, Jace the second and

Seth took the final watch of the night. Lydia and Ross Bennett would start the watches the following night.

The next morning after a quick breakfast of sliced ham on a biscuit, Lydia saddled Chester and moved out toward the west in search of the illegal bootleggers. She rode several miles through rough country. She scanned the horizon frequently looking for tell tale wisps of smoke that might emanate from a working still in operation.

Noon came and she had not found anything resembling a hidden whiskey-making operation. She drew Chester up along a natural spring and let him drink and graze for a while. Lydia took those minutes to sit with a handful of dried apple and a hunk of cheddar for lunch.

A light breeze blew strands of her dark brown hair across her face as she continued to scan the sky in all directions.

Half an hour later, Lydia was back in the saddle and proceeding in a northwesterly direction. She rode for a few miles more before the wind shifted bringing a distinct odor floating in the air. The young woman urged Chester forward faster as the odor grew stronger. On the horizon a thin wisp of smoke rose above the treetops in the distance.

As Chester moved through the thick brush that obscured the ground beyond, Lydia could not see the source. She listened carefully. Hearing no sound of human activity, she dismounted Chester and dropped the reins. The bay stood ground hitched as he always did.

Lydia crept forward through the brush, Winchester at the ready. Peering around an old oak, she observed a lone figure bent over what appeared to be a still in operation. The single male was busy drawing a clear liquid from a tap on the side of a metal kettle. Flames danced brightly underneath the large vessel.

The man with his back to Lydia was Abel Johnson. Johnson had learned the art of blacksmithing as a lad of eighteen. His arms became muscular. His hands were sinewy and bronzed from the hard work at the forge and bellows. Unfortunately accidents at the anvil caused severe burns that left him unable to continue as a smithy.

Now, in his forty-second year, he had turned to another occupation. He had forged stills for acquaintances, learning the details of each component. With a strong desire to regain his independence, he reckoned bootlegging would bring him good money. After all, the amber liquid was coveted by many a man.

Today, Abel hunkered down over the tap to his still to draw his first taste of the day's brew when he heard a twig snap. He stopped, cocked his head to one side and listened intently. Hearing no other movement, he sipped his concoction. It was worthy of his efforts.

Without warning, a lone figure stood up at the edge of the small clearing with a rifle pointed directly at the man. A voice challenged, "Federal Officer! Stand up and turn around slowly! Keep your hands in plain sight!"

Abel straightened to his full height and turned. He could not believe his eyes. A young female dressed in men's clothing stood not fifteen yards from him. Her Winchester was aimed at him. Sunlight caught the Silver Star pinned on the lapel of her jacket.

Abel was so startled that the jar containing the first brew slipped from his hand as he turned. The jar shattered with the whiskey soaking into the dry ground. Abel raised his hands high over his head. "Don't shoot, Missy! I mean no harm!"

Lydia stepped closer to the tall lanky man with strong features. "What is your name?"

"I am Abel Johnson. I live in these woods. I harm no one. What is it that you want?"

"Abel Johnson. I have a warrant for your arrest. The charge is making and selling illegal whiskey in the Indian Territory. Will you come peaceably or do I have to shoot you?"

"I'm always a peaceable man, Missy. I'll mind my manners."

"All right, then. Put out your fire and dump your wares out on the ground."

Abel swallowed the lump in his throat and with tears glistening down his cheek, doused his fire with dirt. He reluctantly opened the tap to the kettle of whiskey. He shook his head as the carefully distilled brew splashed to the ground. He longed for yet another taste before this Marshal would take him away.

Lydia asked a second critical question, "Abel, what do you know of Samuel Booker?"

"Old Sam? Well, he was my partner until about a month ago. Seems he got tired of making whiskey and lit out for the States. I haven't seen hide nor hair of him since."

Lydia nodded. The second warrant could not be served on this trip.

About twilight, Lydia rode into the campsite with Abel Johnson in tow. She was the first back with her quarry. She asked Abel to sit in front of a stout oak tree. She secured him with a lariat around his waist that was tied behind the tree. She offered him a drink from her canteen and he readily accepted. "You are a kind woman, Missy. Thank you."

They made light conversation while they waited for other Marshals to bring in their wanted persons.

Before long, Seth rode into camp with a burly man of sour disposition. Even his bewhiskered face and dirty clothes were overpowered by his strong odor.

Seth was obviously concerned when he saw Lydia with her prisoner. "Lydia, I was hoping that at least one of the other men was back already. Ross and I got all four of our men; however, two of them are wounded. I have to ride back to help Ross bring them in. It should not be more than a couple of hours. Can you handle watching these two by yourself?"

"Yes, Seth. Just tie your man to that tree near Abel there. I'll be alright."

Seth announced loudly so that Joad Mason understood that the female Deputy Marshal would not let her guard down. "Marshal Forsyth, this is Joad Mason. You watch this man carefully. He is a bad one. He is wanted for vicious assault and suspected murder on more than one occasion. You watch him good! Ross and I will return as quickly as we can. God speed the others, we will need them."

After running a rope around Joad's middle that secured around the oak, Seth remounted and rode off into the wilds.

Seth had been gone less than thirty minutes when Joad called out,

"Hey you! You there! Bitch Law Dog! I want some water. It was a dry ride here."

"Watch your mouth, Mason. I won't take any guff from the likes of you." Lydia picked up her canteen and moved toward the outlaw. She reached down to hand him the canteen.

Suddenly, Mason swung his legs around the woman sweeping Lydia off her feet. She was momentarily stunned. Lydia reached for her Colt but he grabbed her arm causing the weapon to fly out of her hand beyond reach of either of them.

Joad stretched out in his ropes and grabbed the young woman by the throat. She swung at him with both fists pounding on his face—attempting to break free.

Joad grabbed one arm before he smacked a meaty fist into the left side of Lydia's face, sending her against the ground. "Now, uppity woman, I'm going to show you how I treat wenches like you!"

The violent man grabbed the front of her shirt, ripping it open to expose her chemise as well as the tops of her breasts. He stared lustily at her white shoulders and heaving breasts. He placed a hand at the top of her chemise to rip it open.

Suddenly, a large sinewy hand grabbed Joad by the throat and squeezed hard. Mason gasped for breath as he released his grip on Lydia. She rolled from his reach as Abel pulled the criminal closer toward him. He doubled his large fist and slugged the distasteful man square in the face. Blood poured from Joad's nose and mouth. His left eye puffed quickly, distorting his vision.

Abel held the man by the throat. He was choking the life out of him. He repeatedly shouted, "You don't hurt, Missy! You don't hurt, Missy! I kill you if you hurt Missy!"

Still on the ground, Lydia shouted, "Abel! Stop it! Damn it, Abel! Unhand that SOB! Leave him alone or I'll have to shoot you!"

The young Marshal frantically took a deep breath, pulled herself to her feet, and quickly retrieved her Colt from where it had fallen. She bolted toward the two men.

Abel had paid Lydia no mind. He continued his rage, throttling the life out of her assailant. Lydia swung her Colt gently against the side of

Abel's head. He shook it off and turned to look into her eyes. Her left eye was slightly swollen and turning color.

Lydia calmly consoled her rescuer, "Abel, I am alright. I am alive. Let that man be."

Abel reluctantly released his grip on the limp perpetrator and rolled off him. Joad continued to cough hard and gasp for air. He slowly curled up like a whipped cur dog and whimpered.

Lydia untied the rope around Abel and bid him to turn the bruised man over. She stuck her knee into the small of Joad's back, wrested his arms behind and cuffed the burly man. Then, she turned to Abel. "Tie his legs together also! I don't want this SOB loose any longer." Abel did as she requested.

"O.K., Abel. I'll not cuff or tie you. You mind your manners and all will be fine."

Lydia went to her saddlebags to retrieve a fresh shirt. She moved behind Chester, using him as a shield to change garments. With regained composure and clean shirt, she joined Abel at the campfire.

The pair made small talk while they waited for the others to join the camp. They did not have to wait long. Jace Williams arrived soon with his two warrants just before Nathan rode in with his two interests.

Lydia gave a quick account of the attempted escape to each returning Marshal to explain Abel's temporary freedom.

Ross and Seth arrived last with their charges. Ross glanced at Lydia, then moved quickly to her. She rose, allowing him to take her hand to lead her behind the picket line. "Just what in Hell happened here?"

"We had a little scuffle. Abel Johnson took care of the situation. He saved my life."

"That does it! I will not leave you alone with vicious men again. You have my word on it!"

"I believe you, Ross. It was yet another lesson for me. I should have tossed the canteen to Mason instead of handing it to him. I'll know better from now on."

Ross looked into Lydia's eyes and she moved to him. He took her into his arms and held her for several long minutes.

"Ross, Abel came to my aid when I was in trouble. He defended me and most likely saved my life. I want to do something for him. I know I cannot let him go, but I want him free of all charges. How do we do this?"

Ross grinned, "You know, I was thinking the same thing. Talk to that court prosecutor that you made friends with. He can withdraw the warrant. If he needs a second person to vouch for it, tell him that I will."

Two days later, the posse of Marshals arrived home in Paris, Texas with their charges. Abel Johnson rode among the prisoners, but he was not cuffed to his saddle horn as the others. When jailers assumed control of the wanted men, one questioned, "Why is this man not handcuffed?"

Lydia replied, "This man will not be cuffed. He is a special situation. Take him to a separate cell and await further instruction."

The following day, Abel Johnson was released from the Federal Jail with a stern warning from Lyle Elliott, the Prosecuting Attorney for the Southern Indian Territory.

"Abel Johnson, I retract your Warrant. Don't cook any more Illegal whiskey in the Indian Territory."

Abel grinned with the advice. There were other places that would want his exceptional elixir and he intended to explore them. He considered the Oklahoma Territory. He intended to profit from those who wanted their whiskey pure, without cheating additives.

CHAPTER TWENTY-ONE

MCALESTER FEDERAL JAIL

Lydia worked with Roseanne in the Marshal's Office for two weeks while her bruised face and black eye healed. Having tasted the excitement of the trails, she was anxious to get back into action with her cohorts.

U.S. Marshal William Franklin drew his mount up to the hitching post in front of the Lamar County Courthouse and dismounted. He wrapped the reins around the post and strode to the entrance. Inside, he moved quickly to his office to find Roseanne and Lydia diligently at work processing the latest wanted warrants, writs, and wanted posters for action.

"Good morning, Roseanne, Marshal Forsyth."

Both women looked up from their desks to return the greeting. Lydia smiled when Franklin looked closely at her wounds and remarked, "Well, you are looking chipper this morning, Forsyth. Would you be ready to take an assignment in the Territory again?"

Lydia perked up considerably at his question. "Yes, Marshal Franklin. I am quite ready for field duty."

"Good! Come in to my office and I'll outline your assignment."

Lydia rose and followed Franklin into his private office. He motioned Lydia to the chair in front of his desk. He sat behind his desk and took out a telegram to peruse once again before speaking.

"Forsyth, I have a request here from Senior Deputy Marshal John Canady. He needs extra guard help for a week or so at the McAlester

Federal Jail. I want you to go there to assist. You will take the train from Sherman tomorrow. You're relieved of office work as of now. Go pack your duffle and get to Sherman.

"Yes, Sir! I'll leave straight away. Thank you, Marshal Franklin."

Lydia chatted briefly with Roseanne, thanking her for the time together while recuperating. She shared the good news with her friend before she departed the office and started down the courthouse hallway.

Marshal Franklin reflected on Lydia's devotion to law and order in the Southern Indian Territory. "She's dedicated to her calling, always willing to do whatever task is given. In the time that she has been a Deputy Marshal, she has traveled the Territory not only with other Officers, but by herself on occasion. She is fearless, an excellent horsewoman and a formidable marksman."

Franklin nodded to himself assuredly, "Yes, Lydia has made several important arrests, served warrants, and writs. She also served as guard at several jails throughout the Territory. She has certainly earned our respect as well as either respect or fear from certain villains and outlaw factions. I made the right choice in appointing her as one of my Deputies."

Lydia left her hotel room at the Peterson Hotel just off the town square and walked downstairs to greet the desk clerk James.

"Good morning, Marshal. You look as if you will take a trip today. When can we expect you back?"

Lydia smiled, "James, I'll be back in a week. My monthly fee has been paid up, yes?"

James returned the smile, "Why, yes, it has. There's no problem."

"Just checking to make sure I've taken care of everything before I leave. Well, I see that the taxi is waiting for me. Good day, James."

Lydia gathered up the Winchester along with her duffle bag and hurried out the door to the waiting vehicle. The driver looked up as Lydia called out, "Good morning, Frank. I need to go to the livery stable for my horse."

Frank Sutton waved a good morning to Lydia as he dismounted from his seat and moved to help with her bag. He quickly appraised Lydia's outfit and knew that she was on another official mission. She wore her men's jeans tucked into riding boots with spurs, dark blue shirt with favorite silk bandana and thigh length dark jacket. He could tell that her Colt was on her hip.

"Well, now. You sure picked a good day for traveling. It looks to be a warm one, though, Marshal Forsyth."

Lydia looked skyward a moment before agreeing with him. "I'm glad, Frank. I like to sight see when I'm out riding."

Once Lydia was situated on the seat next to him, Frank clucked to his team. Half an hour later, Lydia mounted Chester and trotted smartly through the square toward the Sherman Road.

Once out of town, she thought about what lay ahead. Her mind turned somber. "Somewhere along this road close to the cutoff to Garrett's Bluff is where it all happened ten years ago. I will probably pass the location and not even know it." She thought of long ago and her friend Annie Schuler.

Lydia rode easy in the saddle, taking care to be aware of her surroundings. At dusk, she located a shallow stream flowing not far from the road and turned off into the trees along the creek. It seemed a likely place to camp for the night.

She stripped her trappings off Chester and led him down to the water where both horse and rider took advantage of the cool life-giving liquid. Afterward, she made a small camp and spread out her bedroll, laying the Winchester close to hand. Lydia chewed on trail jerky and drank a bit of water from her canteen while Chester grazed close by.

Darkness fell, prompting Lydia to arrange her saddle and bedroll for the night. She listened to the night sounds, identifying the croaking of frogs, the quick scurry of small nocturnal creatures and the occasional hoot of an owl. Satisfied that all was well, she settled into a light sleep. She would be up and in the saddle at daybreak for there were still close to ten or more miles to reach Sherman.

Once in town, she would load Chester in the stock car at the rail depot and continue her journey on the St. Louis and San Francisco Railroad Line, known in these parts as the Frisco Rail Line, to McAlester.

Lydia rode into Sherman before noon, and rode directly to the rail depot. Once there, she stabled Chester in the stock area insuring he was watered and fed. She purposely left his trappings on him, but took her duffle and Winchester rifle with her inside the depot.

She checked with the station agent, inquiring about the next train to her destination. "Hello, Sir, is the two o'clock to McAlester on time?"

The middle-aged man with balding head of hair and wire rimmed spectacles looked up at Lydia. He was surprised to see a young woman dressed in men's clothing. He stammered a bit before replying, "Yes! The McAlester train is on time today. Are you a passenger?"

Lydia smiled as she opened the panel of her jacket to display the Silver Star. "I am Deputy Marshal Forsyth, and yes, I am a ticketed passenger on your train. My horse will be loaded into the stock car. I'll unload him myself if necessary at the end of the trip. Thank you very much for the information."

The agent exhaled, "I'd heard that there were some Lady Marshals, but you are the first one I've seen."

Lydia smiled at the man, then, waved at him before turning toward the interior of the depot. She located a seat where she could observe passengers moving about, then made herself as comfortable on the wooden bench as possible. Within the hour, the agent made a boarding call.

Lydia looked to the stock pen to see Chester being loaded into the stock car. Anxious to travel, Chester went quietly into the rail car with the handler.

Lydia then walked to the last passenger car, climbed up the steps onto the platform and made her way inside. She glanced at the passengers and quickly decided to take the last row facing toward the front of the train.

The seats were typical of the era, a wooden frame and fabric cushions. Lydia settled in and made herself comfortable for the ride. Her duffle and Winchester lay on the seat beside her, under the window.

On schedule, the whistle blew as the wheels of the large steam locomotive spun and caught on the rails. Passengers braced themselves as the train slowly gathered speed. The engineer vigorously rang the bell and blew the whistle once more, announcing the train's departure.

On the north edge of Sherman, the train reached usual passenger train speed of sixty miles per hour. Amazingly, freight trains might travel to nearly one hundred miles per hour. Lydia watched out the window as the landscape flew past her view. She reminisced of her rail rides as a child. She remembered those rides when she traveled much slower.

Technical advances, coupled with society's desire to travel faster and further, meant a shorter ride. After all, this was the 1890's and the turn of the century was within a decade.

Lydia was pleased with the freedom to ponder life in North Texas and the Indian Territory in this final decade of the nineteenth century. She thought, "What will life be like at the turn of century? Will I remain a Deputy Marshal working out of Paris? Will statehood be an option for Oklahoma? The Indian Territory? Will outlaws still abound?" She pondered these questions as the terrain changed.

Crossing the river was a sign for her to lean back against her seat and close her eyes. A short nap would do her good.

Several hours later, the Frisco Line arrived in McAlester with whistle blowing, bells ringing, and the hard reversal of wheels to finally bring the train to a stop along the station house. Hot steam belched from the engine.

Lydia stood quickly from the seat, stretched a bit, and gathered her belongings. She walked to the front of the car and disembarked as the last passenger in the car. Once on the platform, she moved to the stock car to watch handlers install the loading platform. She smiled as Chester allowed himself to be lead out of the rail car and into the stock corral adjacent to the station house.

Lydia heard a familiar voice from behind her. She turned to face the tall, lanky figure of John Canady. Canady had a twinkle in his brown eyes as he grinned and held out his hand to one of his favorite Deputy Marshals.

"Lydia! Why, Missy, it has been many a moon since we've seen you here in McAlester. I'm glad that Franklin sent you here to help out. Naturally, Katherine and I expect you to stay with us, rather than the local hotel. Katherine will have a fine supper for us when we get home."

Canady, ever jovial, continued, "I suppose you brought that wild thing you call Chester with you?"

Lydia countered with, "Well, John, Chester has mellowed, and yes, he has been off-loaded and placed in the depot corral."

"I brought a buckboard wagon to carry us home. I'll take your duffle. I don't suppose you'd trust me with that Winchester."

Lydia laughed, "Not likely! I'll hang on to it. Here's my duffle. I'll meet you in front of the depot with Chester."

Canady took Lydia's baggage and walked to the front of the rail depot where his buckboard with matched sorrels stood patiently waiting for him. He placed Lydia's bag in the bed of the wagon, then stood with his horses for a bit.

Several minutes later, Lydia emerged from the alleyway between the depot and the holding corral. Chester plodded along beside her, reins looped over the saddle horn. She tied his reins to the rear of the Canady wagon.

"Here we are, John. Let's be off to your home. I'm anxious to see Katherine, and yes, I'm hankering for her home cooked meals."

Canady waited until Lydia climbed up on the seat next to him. He slapped reins lightly to his team's back and turned the wagon toward his home.

Katherine Canady was a slender woman with auburn hair. Her Scottish ancestry was obvious. She had been excited to learn that Franklin had chosen Lydia to serve in McAlester for a spell.

Lydia and John found Katherine flitting around her kitchen making ready last minute details before supper. The roasted chicken, boiled potatoes, and carrots from her garden were ready. Supper sat on the cast iron stove near the table set for three. She could think of a hundred things to talk with Lydia about.

Katherine looked out the kitchen window as she'd done frequently for the last hour and saw with delight that John and Lydia drove up in the buckboard. She rushed out the back door to meet with them. The two women embraced one another with a hug and a kiss to the cheek.

"Welcome to our home, Lydia. I've got a nice supper ready for us. I'll get it ready for the table while you care for your animal and settle in."

The next morning, Lydia and John Canady rode their horses to the McAlester Federal Jail. John introduced her to his current guards before escorting her into the cell block where he made an announcement to the prisoners.

"All right, gents. Pay attention! This here is Deputy Marshal Forsyth. She will be one of your guards for a few days. Do as she says and mind your manners."

Canady and Lydia walked the cellblock as he indentified each man and shared the violations. There were comments from the prisoners as they observed the attractive Lady Marshal.

"Oh yah! A good looking guard for a change!"

"You going to make us mind our manners, Missy?"

"I been a bad man. Come over here and spank me, pretty lady."

Lydia was not amused by the comments. She addressed the crowd. "You men take heed. I expect good behavior and cooperation. In case you think I am soft, I will tell you this. I know how to use this Colt on my hip. Thank you for your attention."

One of the prisoners blurted out, "She ain't lying! I read in the newspaper that she has shot men who resisted arrest. I don't intend to be the next one."

And, so it went. The prisoners did as Lydia bid. There were no more catcalls or lewd remarks.

CHAPTER TWENTY-TWO

JUSTICE

On her fourth day at the McAlester Federal Jail, Lydia decided that she would take a break to visit J.J. McAlester's Store. She looked smart in a maroon riding suit with cream colored blouse buttoned at the neck. The Silver Star was on her lapel, her Colt slung on her left hip, butt forward.

The young Officer made her way to the stable where she saddled Chester. She rode to the center of town and tied up at the hitching rack in front of the general store. Stepping up on the boardwalk, she entered the establishment. Of special interest to Lydia was the area in the rear of the store devoted to clothing for women.

She glanced around the store to take in the clientele. Two men were considering rifles and revolvers in glass cases. A trio of old timers sat in wooden chairs around the potbellied stove munching on samples of fresh crackers as they sipped on a cool beverage. They spoke of the weather and politics as usual.

The old gentlemen looked up curiously at this lady Deputy Marshal, who had come to buy herself something. They had heard the town gossips describing her.

Lydia especially took notice of what interested the women customers. One woman monopolized the clerk asking to examine several pieces of jewelry. Another female shopper clutched a Butterick dress pattern that she planned to purchase. Methodically, she unrolled several bolts of cloth to feel the fabric and make note of the design.

A gentleman with grey hair and trim mustache and beard stood at a front counter discussing a legal document with a clerk. He was well dressed in a dark suit and maroon vest. His vest pocket held a watch on a gold chain. The chain was attached to a fob looped through a vest button. A small bulge under the man's jacket indicated a weapon on his right hip.

Lydia glanced at the fellow and considered that he was well dressed for daytime in McAlester. She dismissed the idea as she continued through the store to browse the counter now void of the obnoxious woman who had obviously looked at every piece of jewelry in the case.

Looking over the selection, she overheard the conversation between the clerk and well-dressed gentleman.

The clerk advised, "Sir, this application requires your name."

"Thomas G. Woodard."

"Mr. Woodard, I apologize, but I need your full name. What does the "G" stand for?"

"My full name is Thomas *Gabriel* Woodard."

At the sound of the name *Gabriel*, Lydia's heart quickened. She turned slowly to look at the man as if truly seeing him for the very first time. She looked him up and down very carefully. Her eyes became riveted on the gold watch chain and fob.

She stood in awe. Mr. Woodard's watch fob looked very familiar to her. Her thoughts turned immediately to ten years previous. She must make sure of her suspicions.

Lydia quietly approached the men and spoke directly to the gentleman. "Good afternoon, Sir. I was just admiring your watch fob. It seems quite unusual. May I see it?"

Woodard casually glanced at Lydia and obviously flattered, nodded, "Yes." He reached down and withdrew the watch and chain from his vest, handing it to her for examination. She smiled at him.

The fob was a girl's locket. Lydia deftly opened the locket and stared intently. Her heart beat rapidly as she closed the locket and returned the watch and fob back to Woodard.

"The young girl is quite lovely."

"Thank you. She is my niece. It was a gift from her several years ago. It is a keepsake for me."

Lydia turned away from Woodard. She walked some eight or ten paces and turned around abruptly to face Woodard.

The young woman's eyes blazed with anger and hurt, yet she remained composed. She took a deep breath.

"Gabe!"

The man spun around to face Lydia. For the first time, he took notice of the Silver Star on her jacket. Her hand hovered over the butt of her Colt.

Startled customers dived behind counters, falling to the floor. The old gents at the potbellied stove scrambled to a corner behind large barrels of bulk food.

Woodard's hand moved swiftly to the butt of his revolver.

"Federal Officer! You are under arrest for murder! Drop that gun!"

"Like Hell!"

His hand swiftly drew the revolver from the holster and lined up to fire at the young Marshal.

Lydia's hand moved like a striking rattler. Her Colt leveled and spit flame and hot lead. The first bullet smacked into Gabe's chest. He staggered back a step and struggled to line up on Lydia once again.

Her left palm fanned the Colt hammer just as Seth had taught her, amid terrified screams from other customers. She fired once, twice, three times. All four bullets hit Gabe in a tight circle.

His finger tightened against his trigger and, as he fell, fired into the ceiling of McAlester's store. His battered body fell backward into the corner of a counter, shattering the glass display case. The revolver slid from his hand across the floor.

Lydia held the smoking Colt as she approached Gabe. He gasped for air.

"How did you know?" he stammered, eyes wide. Blood flowed from the four bullet holes in his chest and rapidly pooled on the floor.

"The picture in the locket is not your niece. The girl in the locket is me! I gave that locket to Annie Schuler the day before you murdered her and her family."

Gabe's eyes blinked and his face twitched before he took his last breath. Lydia knelt beside the man and pulled the lids over his eyes. She then removed the gold watch, chain, and precious locket from Gabe's body.

Shoppers were slow to move about the store. Once on foot, several moved to see who had been shot by the Lady Marshal; others just wanted out of the store and to the safety of their homes.

Momentarily, the McAlester Sheriff and two deputies entered the store with guns drawn. Lydia turned to face them. She quickly identified herself. "Sheriff, I am Deputy Marshal Forsyth. This man, Thomas Gabriel Woodard, known to his gang as "Gabe", has had a murder warrant on him for the past ten years. I finally identified him and challenged him. He went for his gun and I was forced to shoot him. I assure you that I carry a warrant authorizing me to arrest him."

The Sheriff acknowledged her information. "I understand completely Marshal Forsyth. We have been trying to figure out who this "Gabe" was for quite some time. We will take over here, Marshal Forsyth. You may return to your responsibilities at the Federal Jail.

Two days later, Lydia boarded the train back to Sherman, Texas. In her pocket was Annie's locket and chain.

Upon her return to Paris, Lydia reported in to Marshal Franklin. She recounted the gunfight with Thomas Gabriel Woodard, known as "Gabe" to his gang of outlaws.

Franklin was without words for a while. He recalled reading an old newspaper account of the Schuler family murder on the road to Sherman. While the murders took place ten years earlier, and before his arrival in Paris, local authorities had appraised him of the cold case.

The veteran lawman spoke to his young Deputy, "Marshal Forsyth, you are to be commended for your quick action and bravery in the line of duty. The citizens of Paris deserve to know that justice has been served."

The following Saturday, Lydia Forsyth arose early and relaxed in a tub of lavender bubble bath before taking care to style her hair in a smart coif. She dressed in a newly purchased pale blue silk gown and placed her mother's cameo broach on a matching velvet ribbon at her neck.

She rode to the cemetery with purpose on this morning. Leaving the buggy, she took a ground cloth, a hand shovel, and a small sealed tin and walked toward graves she had visited years ago. There, she dug a small hole next to the headstone of Annie Schuler. Once Lydia had placed the tin in the hole and covered it with soil, she stood and retrieved the ground cloth and shovel.

Lydia stood in silence near the headstone of her best friend from childhood for a few moments. She smiled as she recalled the fond memories they shared before Annie was taken from her. The young woman bowed her head in prayer.

Brilliant sunlight broke through an overcast sky just as Lydia wiped away tears. She turned to walk back to Ross Bennett who waited for her. Ross was attired in his best Sunday suit. He helped her into the buggy and then climbed in beside her.

"Are you ready for this?"

Lydia moved closer to Ross for a tender kiss.

"Yes, Ross. Let's get to the church. The preacher and many friends are waiting for us."

Ross laughed, "I don't think they will start anything without us." Lydia snuggled yet closer to him as the buggy moved slowly out of the cemetery.

As Lydia and Ross faded from view, the translucent apparition of a young girl with blonde hair appeared next to her headstone. She was smiling and waving farewell to the departing couple on their wedding day. Around her neck was a friendship heart locket on a gold chain.